HAL•LEONARD

GUITAR

PLAY-ALONG

CLASSIC PUNK

VOL. 102

T0081963

ISBN 978-1-4234-4325-4

HAL•LEONARD®
CORPORATION

7777 W. BLUEMOUND RD. P.O. BOX 13819 MILWAUKEE, WI 53213

Visit Hal Leonard Online at
www.halleonard.com

CONTENTS

Guitar Notation Legend

THE MUSICAL STAFF shows pitches and rhythms and is divided by bar lines into measures. Pitches are named after the first seven letters of the alphabet.

TABLATURE graphically represents the guitar fingerboard. Each horizontal line represents a string, and each number represents a fret.

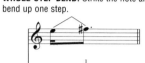
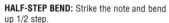

4th string, 2nd fret — 1st & 2nd strings open, played together — open D chord

HALF-STEP BEND: Strike the note and bend up 1/2 step.

WHOLE-STEP BEND: Strike the note and bend up one step.

GRACE NOTE BEND: Strike the note and immediately bend up as indicated.

SLIGHT (MICROTONE) BEND: Strike the note and bend up 1/4 step.

BEND AND RELEASE: Strike the note and bend up as indicated, then release back to the original note. Only the first note is struck.

PRE-BEND: Bend the note as indicated, then strike it.

VIBRATO: The string is vibrated by rapidly bending and releasing the note with the fretting hand.

PALM MUTING: The note is partially muted by the pick hand lightly touching the string(s) just before the bridge.

HAMMER-ON: Strike the first (lower) note with one finger, then sound the higher note (on the same string) with another finger by fretting it without picking.

PULL-OFF: Place both fingers on the notes to be sounded. Strike the first note and without picking, pull the finger off to sound the second (lower) note.

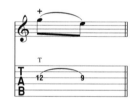

LEGATO SLIDE: Strike the first note and then slide the same fret-hand finger up or down to the second note. The second note is not struck.

SHIFT SLIDE: Same as legato slide, except the second note is struck.

TRILL: Very rapidly alternate between the notes indicated by continuously hammering on and pulling off.

TAPPING: Hammer ("tap") the fret indicated with the pick-hand index or middle finger and pull off to the note fretted by the fret hand.

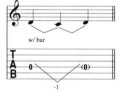

NATURAL HARMONIC: Strike the note while the fret-hand lightly touches the string directly over the fret indicated.

PINCH HARMONIC: The note is fretted normally and a harmonic is produced by adding the edge of the thumb or the tip of the index finger of the pick hand to the normal pick attack.

TREMOLO PICKING: The note is picked as rapidly and continuously as possible.

VIBRATO BAR DIVE AND RETURN: The pitch of the note or chord is dropped a specified number of steps (in rhythm), then returned to the original pitch.

VIBRATO BAR SCOOP: Depress the bar just before striking the note, then quickly release the bar.

VIBRATO BAR DIP: Strike the note and then immediately drop a specified number of steps, then release back to the original pitch.

Additional Musical Definitions

(accent) • Accentuate note (play it louder).

(staccato) • Play the note short.

D.S. al Coda • Go back to the sign (𝄋), then play until the measure marked "***To Coda***," then skip to the section labelled "**Coda**."

D.C. al Fine • Go back to the beginning of the song and play until the measure marked "***Fine***" (end).

Fill • Label used to identify a brief melodic figure which is to be inserted into the arrangement.

N.C. • Harmony is implied.

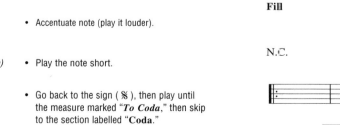

• Repeat measures between signs.

• When a repeated section has different endings, play the first ending only the first time and the second ending only the second time.

California Sun

Words and Music by Morris Levy and Henry Glover

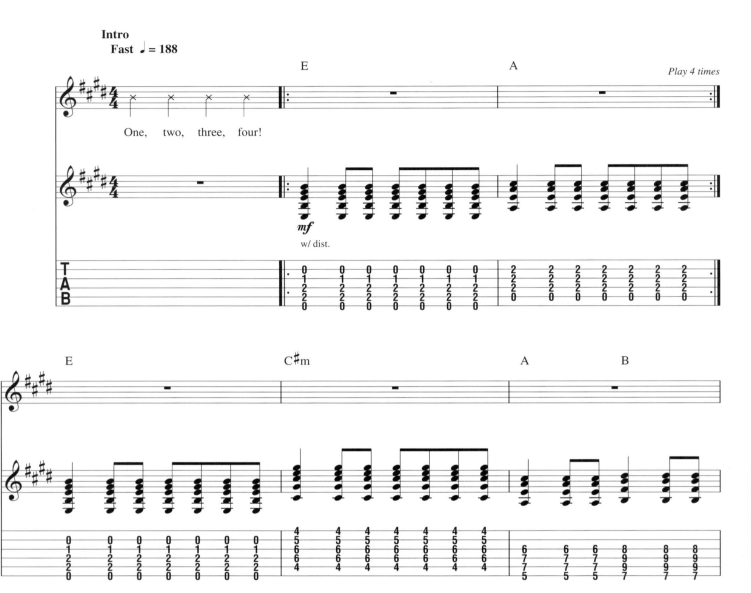

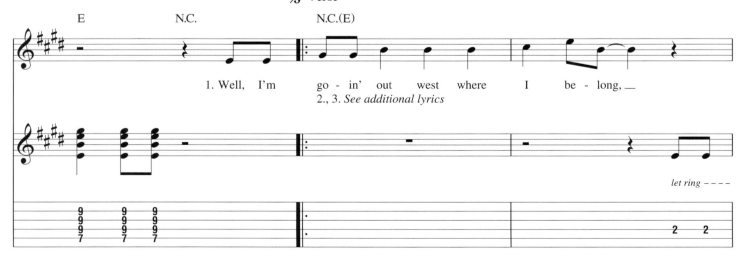

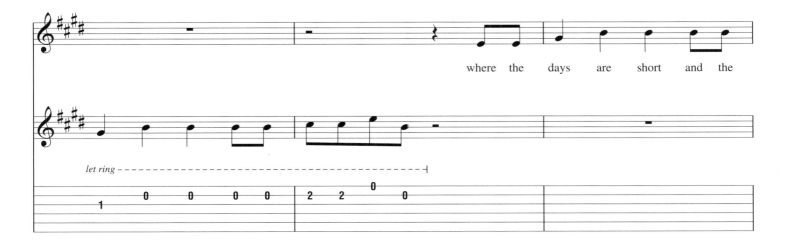

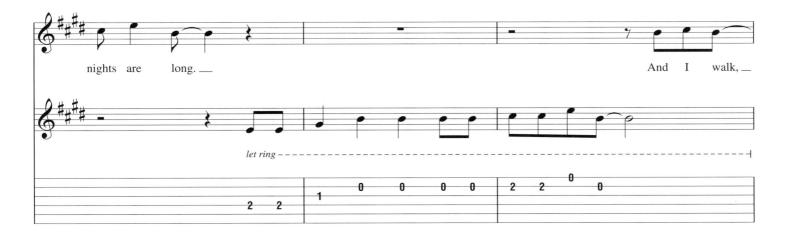

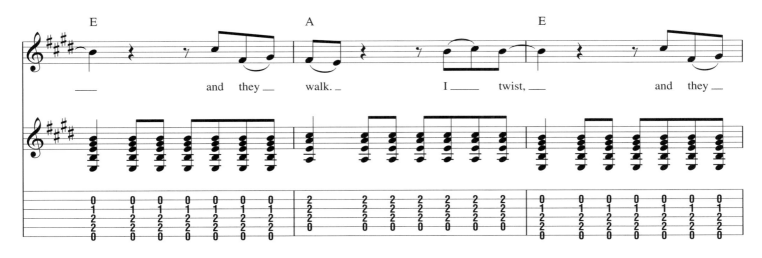

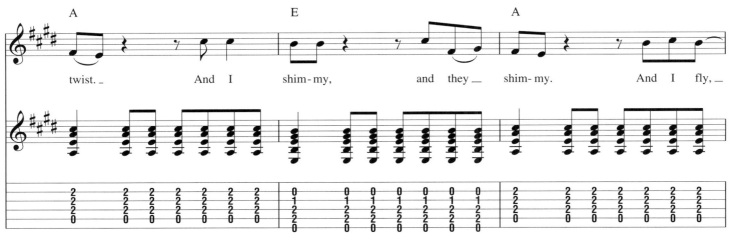

7

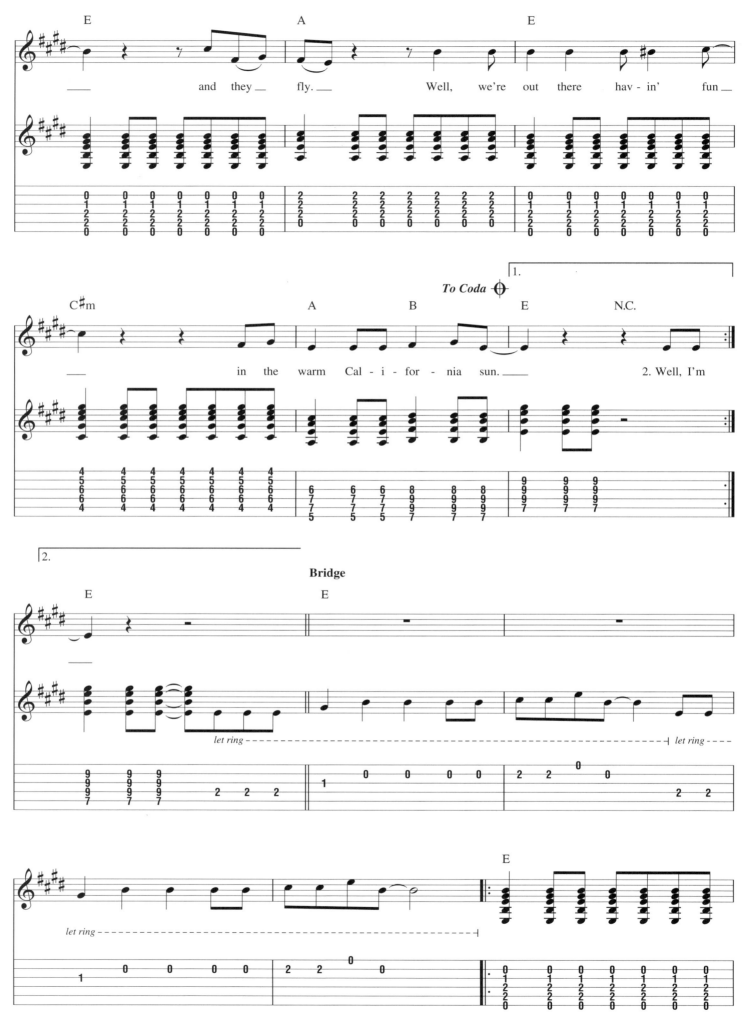

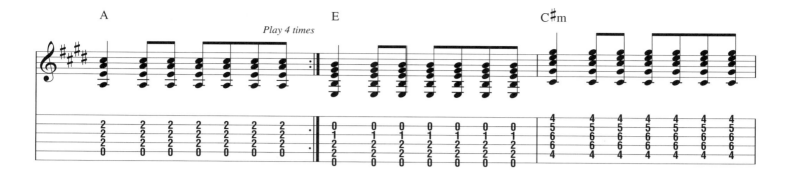

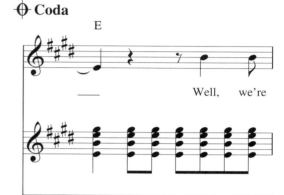

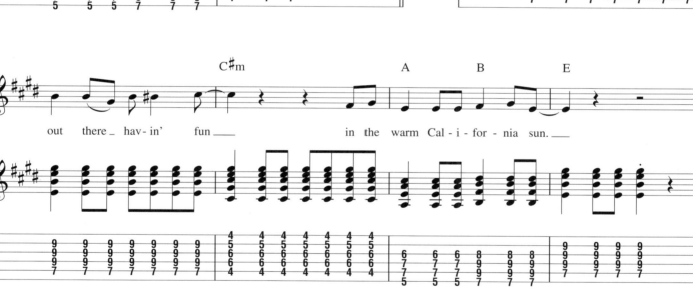

Additional Lyrics

2. Well, I'm goin' out west down on the coast
   Where the California girls are really the most.
   And I walk, and they walk. I twist, and they twist.
   And I shimmy, and they shimmy. And I fly, and they fly.
   Well, we're out there havin' fun in the warm California sun.

3. Well, the girls are frisky in old Frisco.
   A pretty little chick wherever you go.
   Oh, and I walk, and they walk. I twist, and they twist.
   And I shimmy, and they shimmy. And I fly, and they fly.
   Well, we're out there havin' fun in the warm California sun.
   Well, we're out there havin' fun in the warm California sun.

God Save the Queen

**Words and Music by Paul Thomas Cook, Stephen Philip Jones,
Glen Matlock and John Lydon**

1. God save the queen. ____
2. *See additional lyrics*

The fas-cist re - gime. ____

They

Pre-Chorus

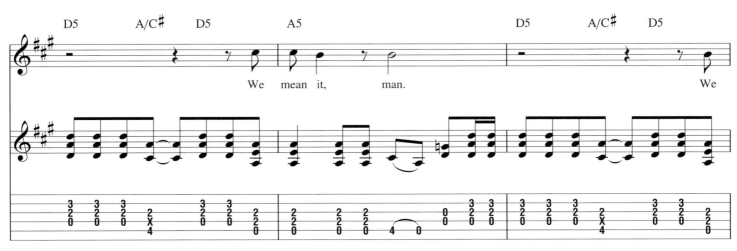

love our queen. _____ God saves. _____

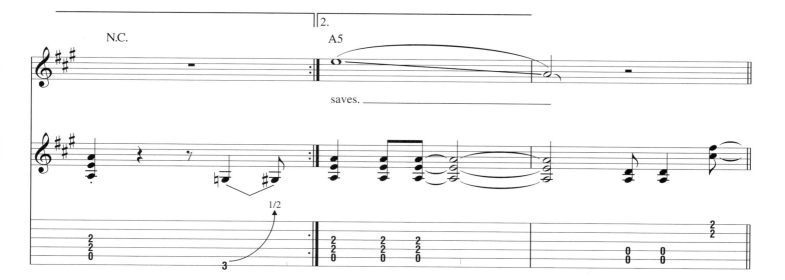

saves. _____

Guitar Solo

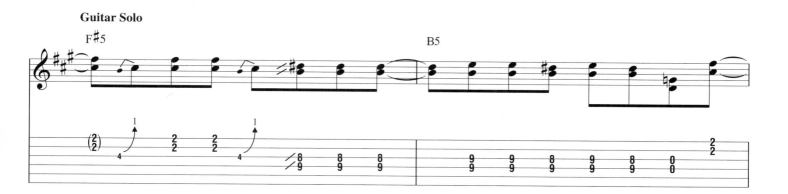

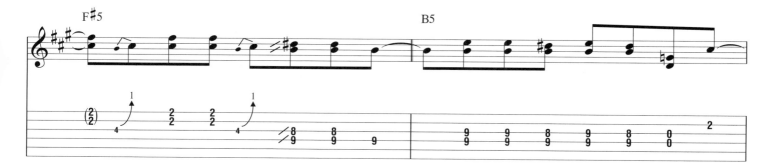

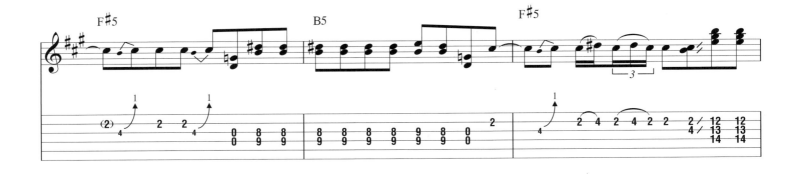

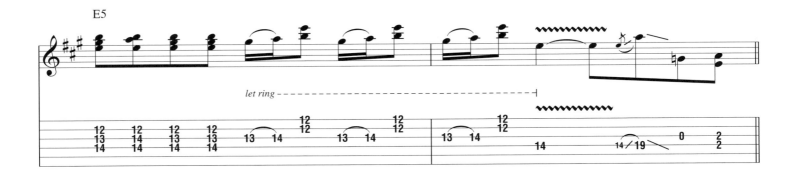

Chorus

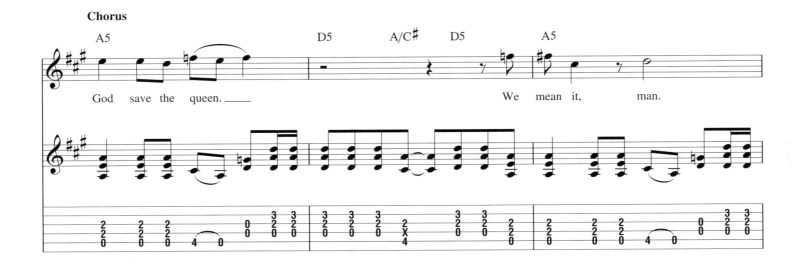

God save the queen. We mean it, man.

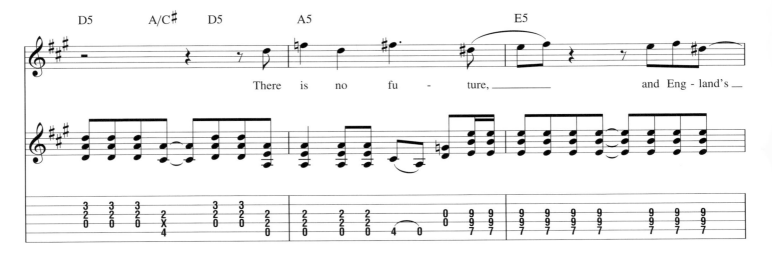

There is no fu-ture, and Eng-land's

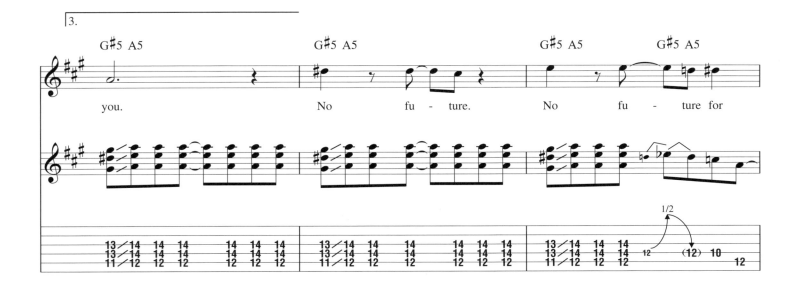

you.　　　　　No　　fu - ture.　　　No　　fu - ture for

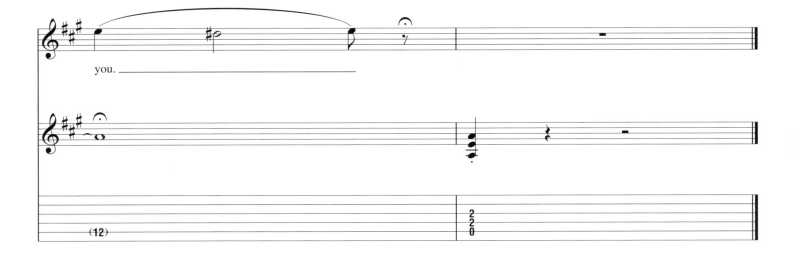

you.

Additional Lyrics

2. God save the Queen.
   Those tourists are money.
   And our figure head is not what she seems.
   Oh, God save history.
   God save your mad parade.
   Oh, Lord, God have mercy.
   All crimes are paid.

Pre-Chorus 2. Oh, when there's no future how can there be sin?
   We're the flowers in your dustbin.
   We're the poison in your human machine.
   We're the future. Your future.

Holiday in Cambodia

Words and Music by Bruce Slesinger, Darren Henley, East Bay Ray, Jello Biafra and Klaus Flouride

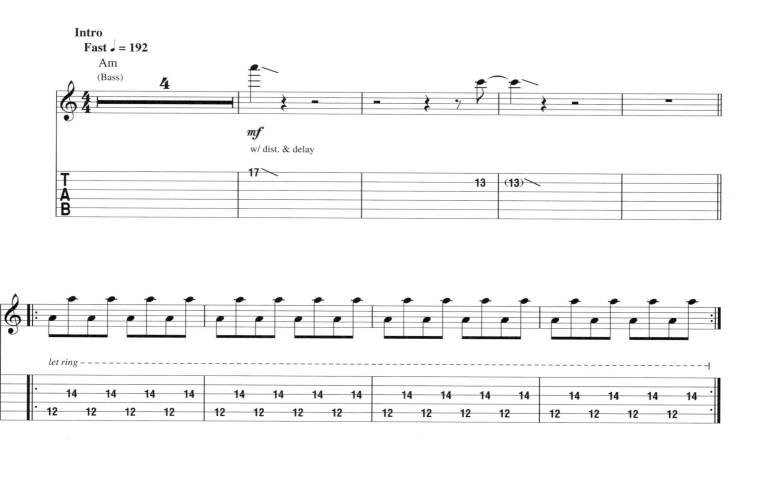

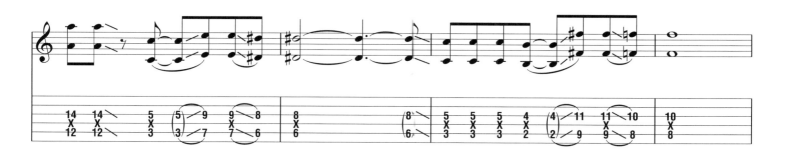

1. So, you

Verse

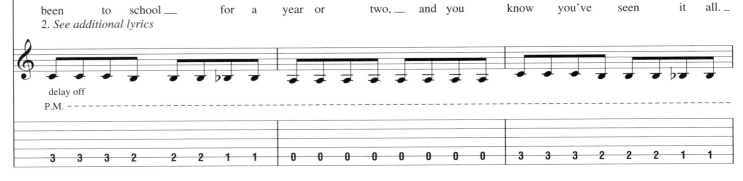

been to school ___ for a year or two, ___ and you know you've seen it all. ___
2. See additional lyrics

delay off
P.M. -

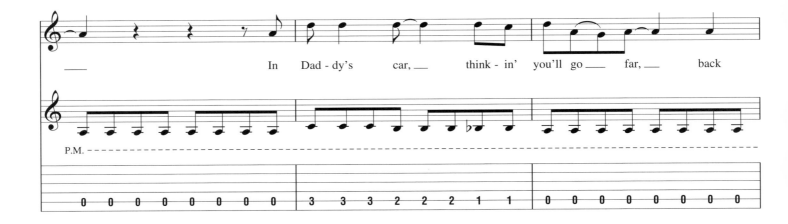

In Dad - dy's car, ___ think - in' you'll go ___ far, ___ back

P.M. -

G

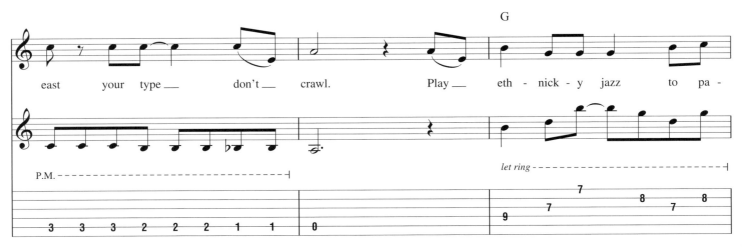

east your type ___ don't ___ crawl. Play ___ eth - nick - y jazz to pa -

P.M. - |

let ring -

rade your snazz on your five - grand ste - re - o. _____

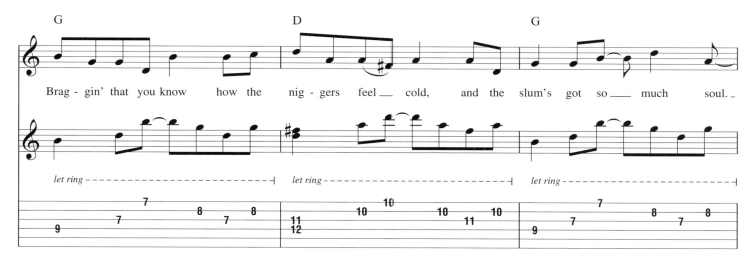

Brag - gin' that you know how the nig - gers feel __ cold, and the slum's got so __ much soul. _

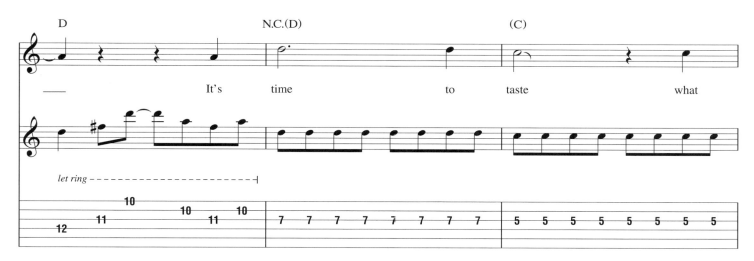

_____ It's time to taste what

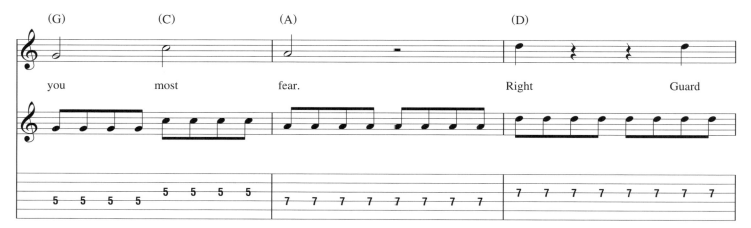

you most fear. Right Guard

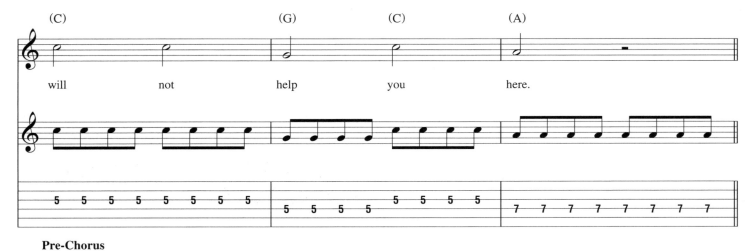

will   not   help   you   here.

Pre-Chorus

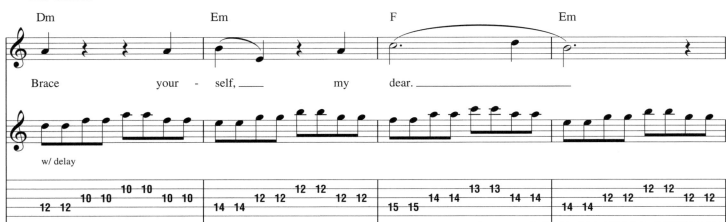

Brace   your - self, ___   my   dear. ___

w/ delay

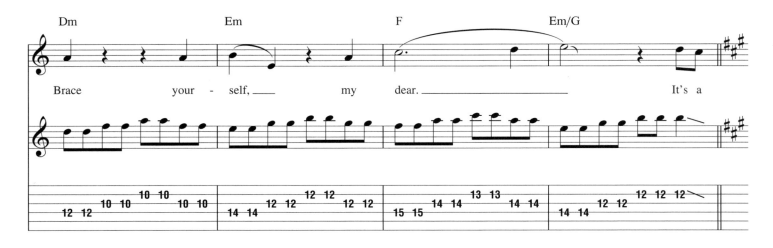

Brace   your - self, ___   my   dear. ___   It's a

Chorus

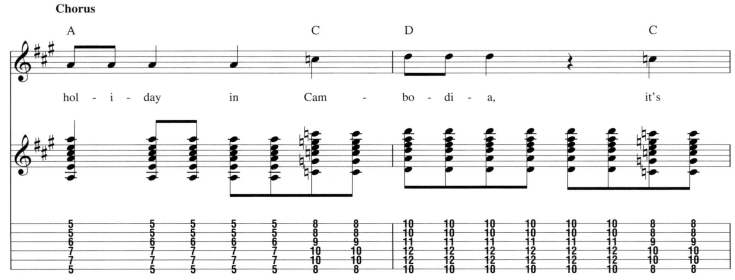

hol - i - day   in   Cam - bo - di - a,   it's

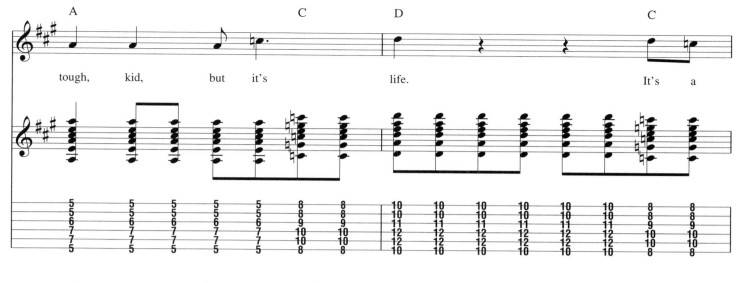

tough, kid, but it's life. It's a

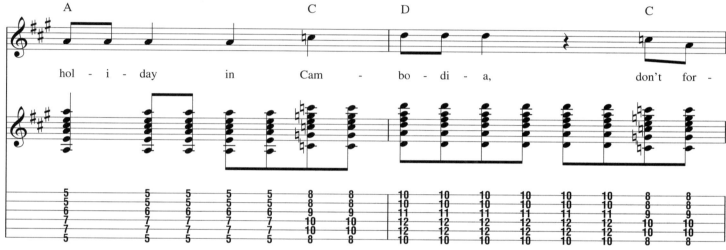

hol - i - day in Cam - bo - di - a, don't for -

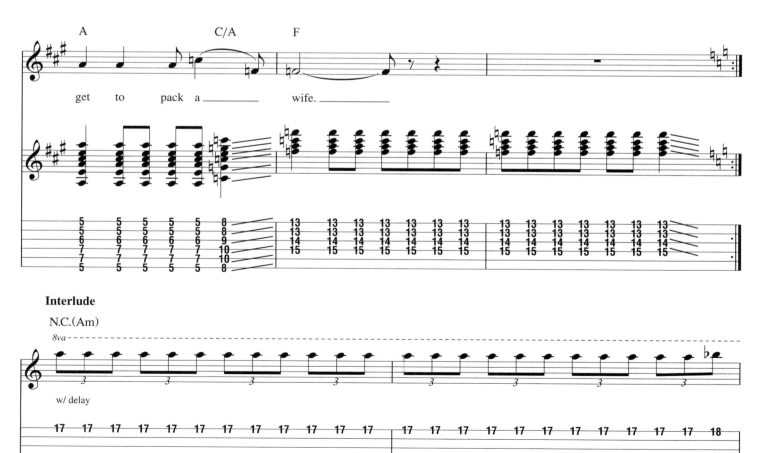

get to pack a _____ wife. _____

Interlude

N.C.(Am)

w/ delay

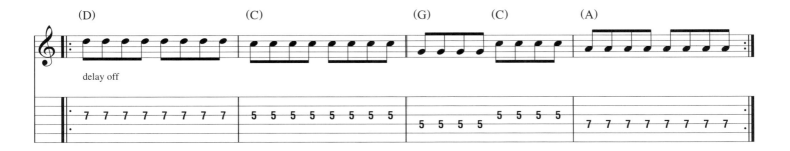

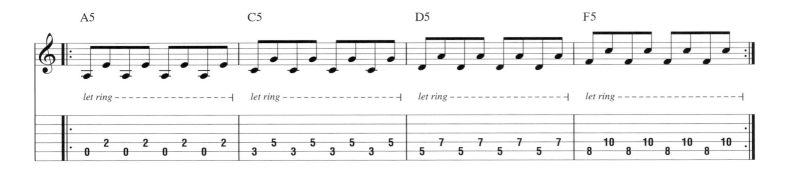

Bridge

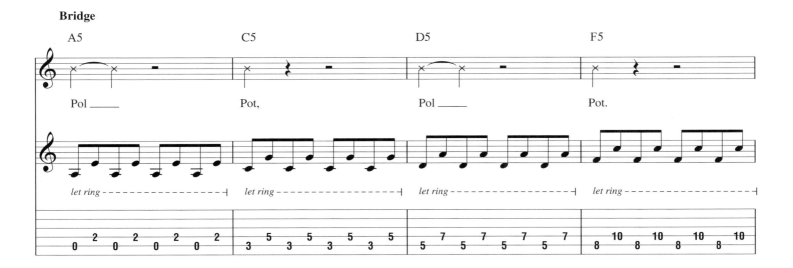

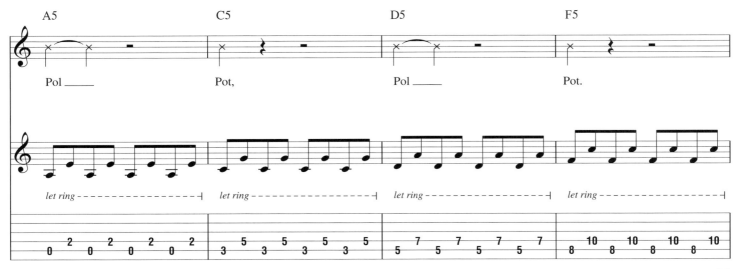

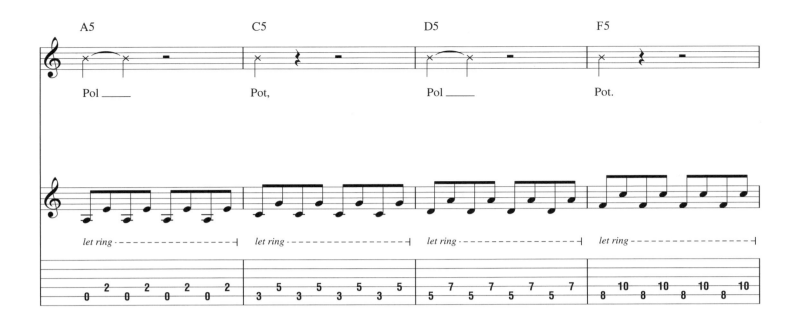

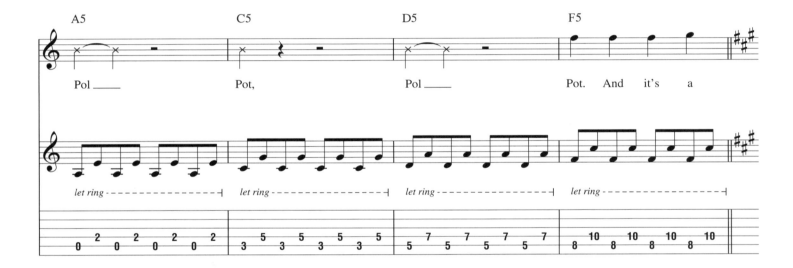

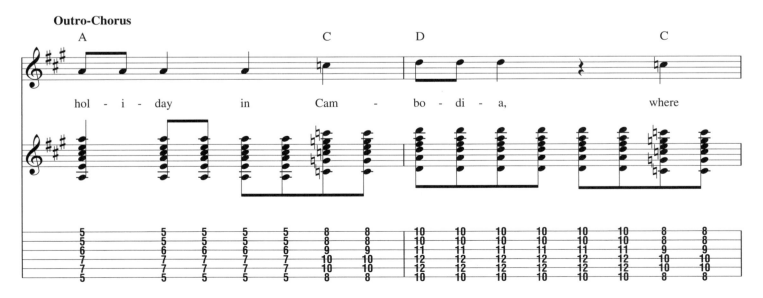

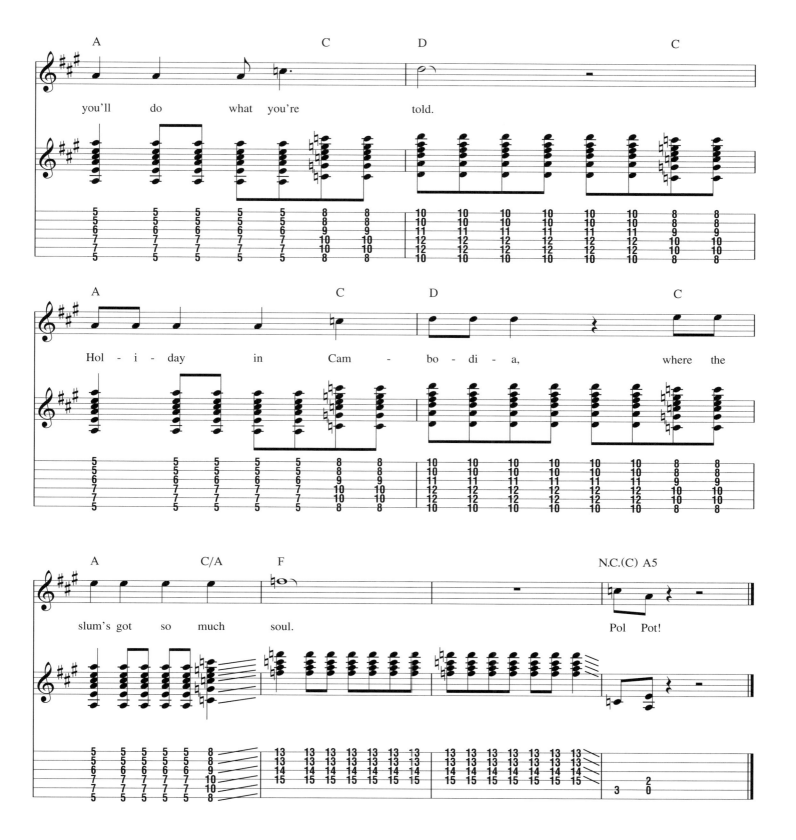

Additional Lyrics

2. You're a star belly sneech, you suck like a leech, you want everyone to act like you.
Kiss ass while you bitch so you can get rich, but your boss gets richer off you.
Well, you'll work harder with a gun in your back for a bowl of rice a day.
Slave for soldiers 'til you starve, then your head is skewered on a stake.
Now you can go where people are one.
Now you can go where they get things done.

Pre-Chorus 2. What you need, my son, what you need my son is a...

Chorus 2. Holiday in Cambodia, where people dress in black.
Need a holiday in Cambodia, where you'll kiss ass or crack.

25

In a Free Land

Words and Music by Bob Mould

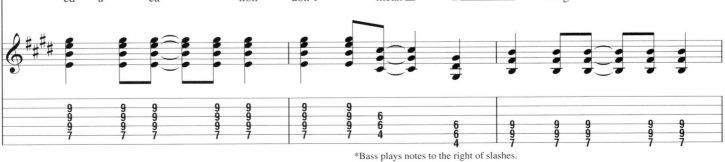

*Bass plays notes to the right of slashes.

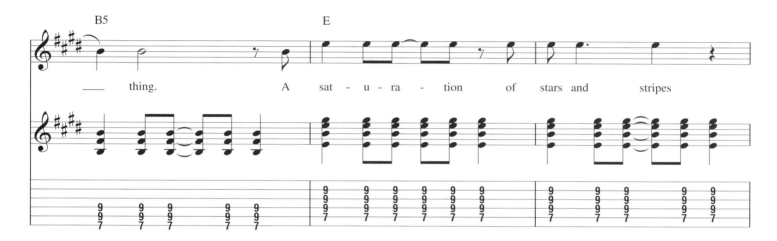

Interlude

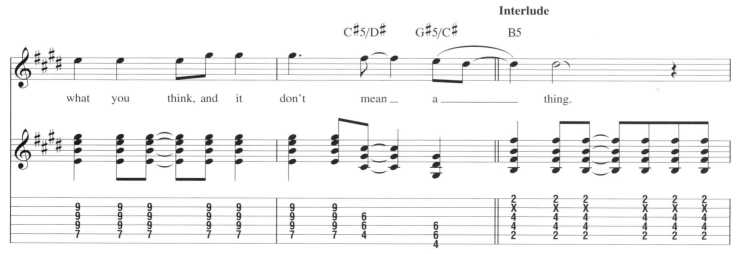

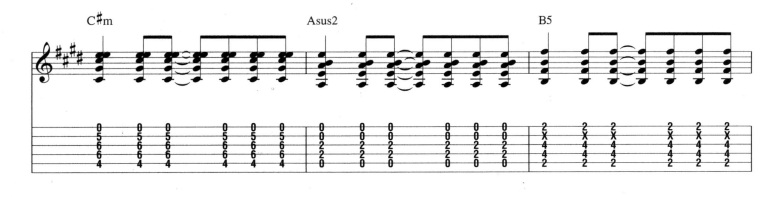

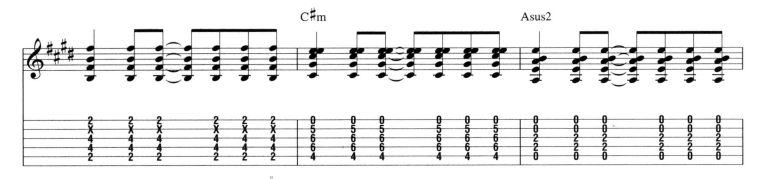

𝄋 Chorus

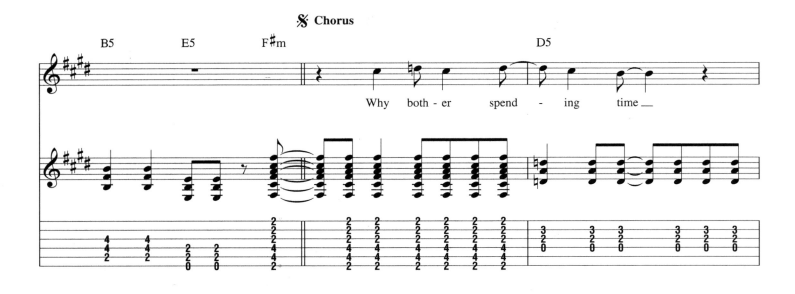

Why both- er spend - ing time ___

read - ing up on ___ things?

Ev - 'ry- bod- y's an au-

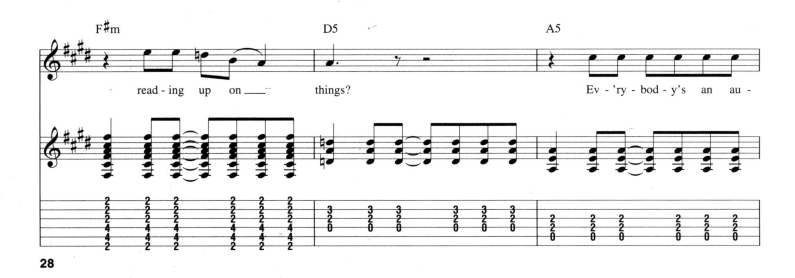

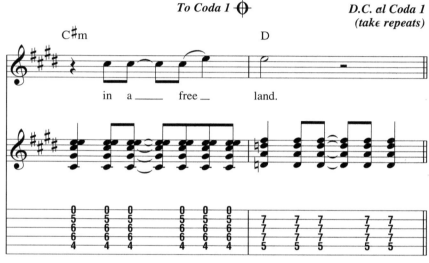

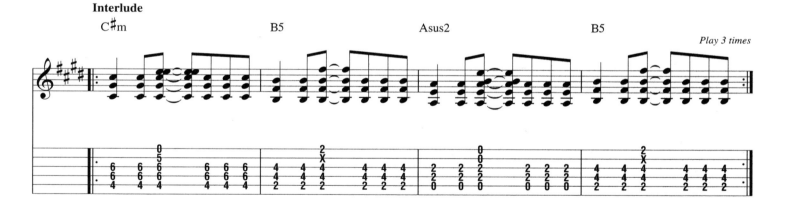

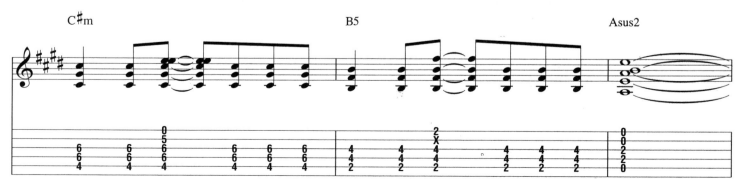

Guitar Solo

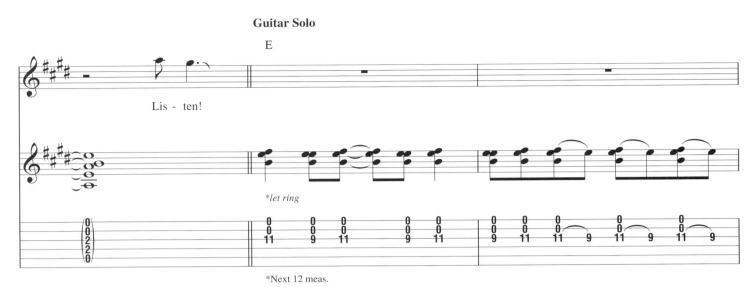

Lis - ten!

*let ring

*Next 12 meas.

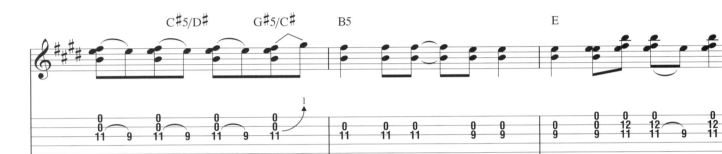

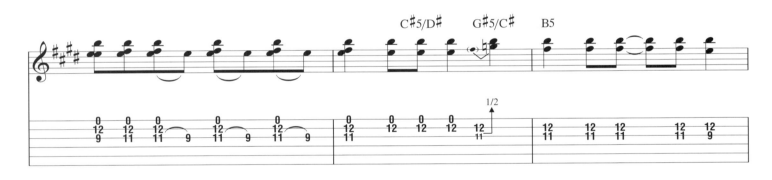

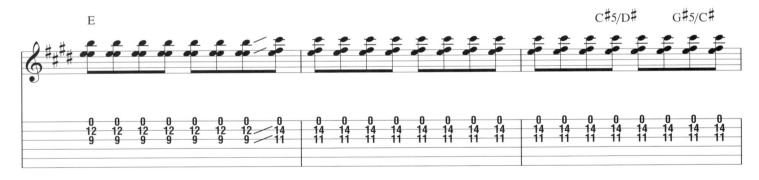

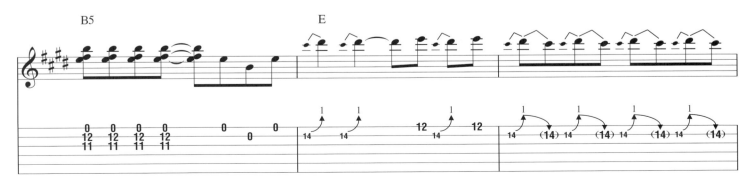

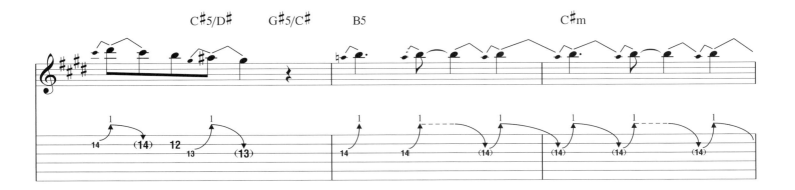

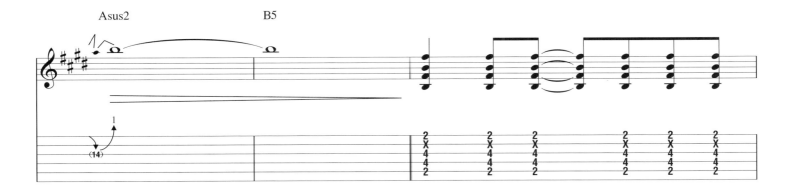

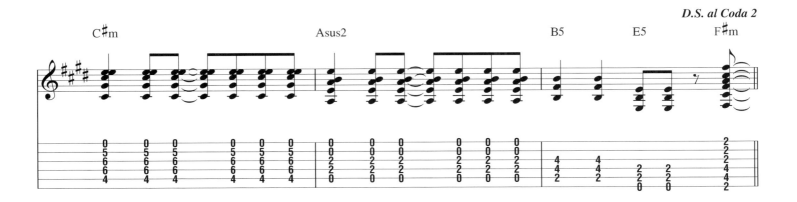

Coda 2

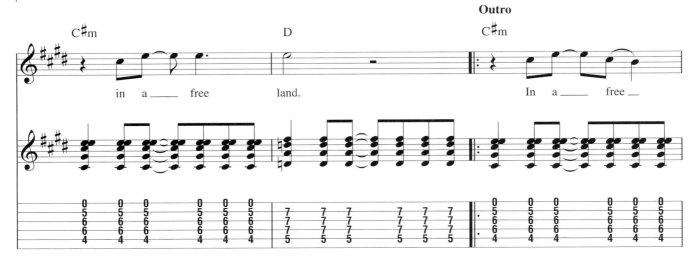

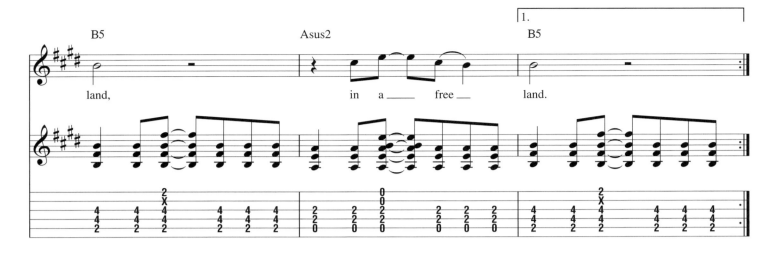

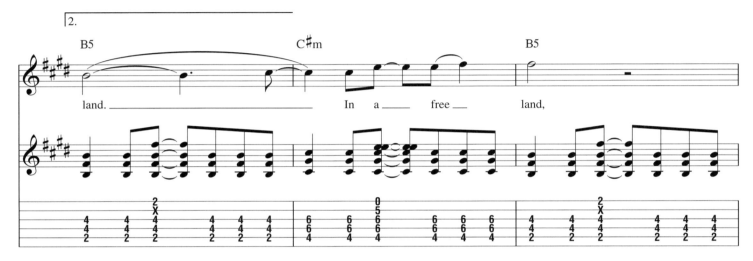

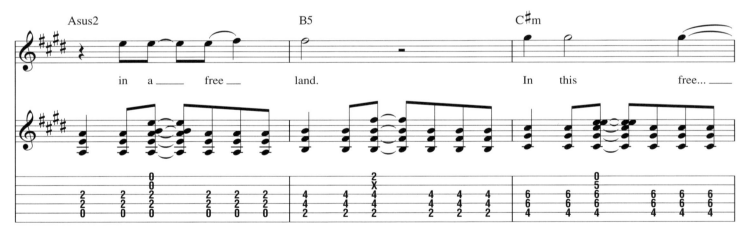

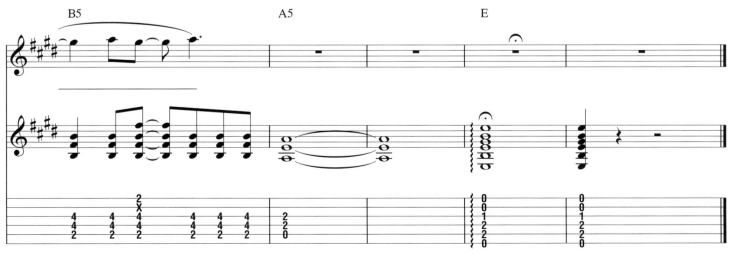

Institutionalized

Words and Music by Amery Smith, Louiche Mayorga and Mike Muir

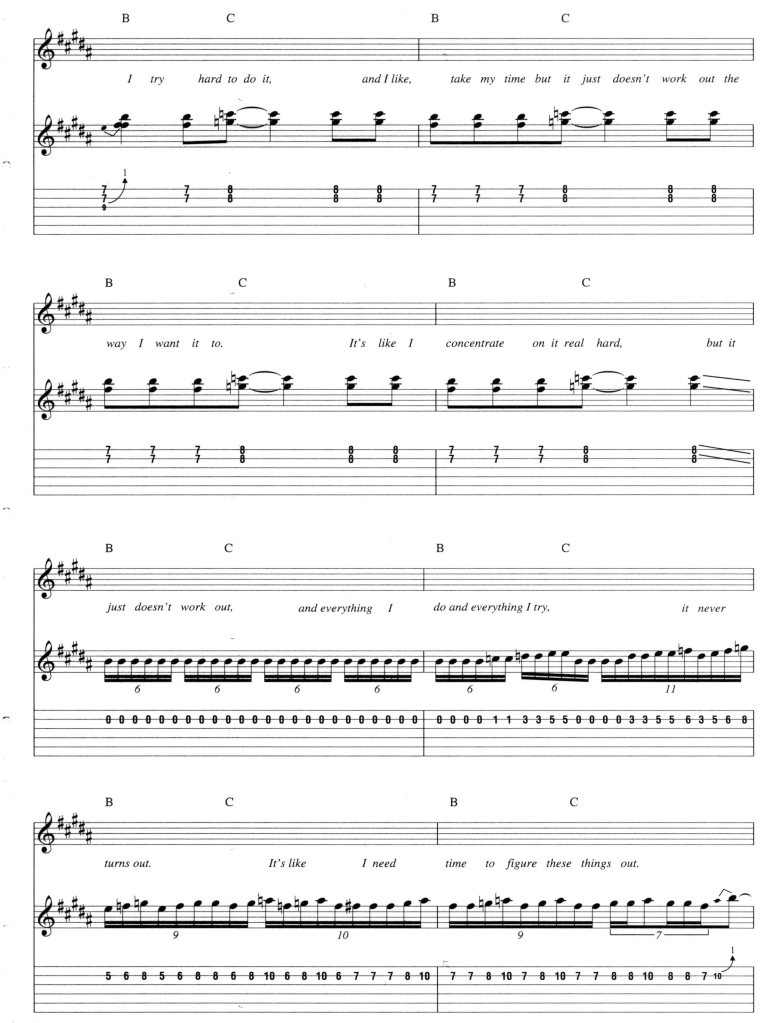

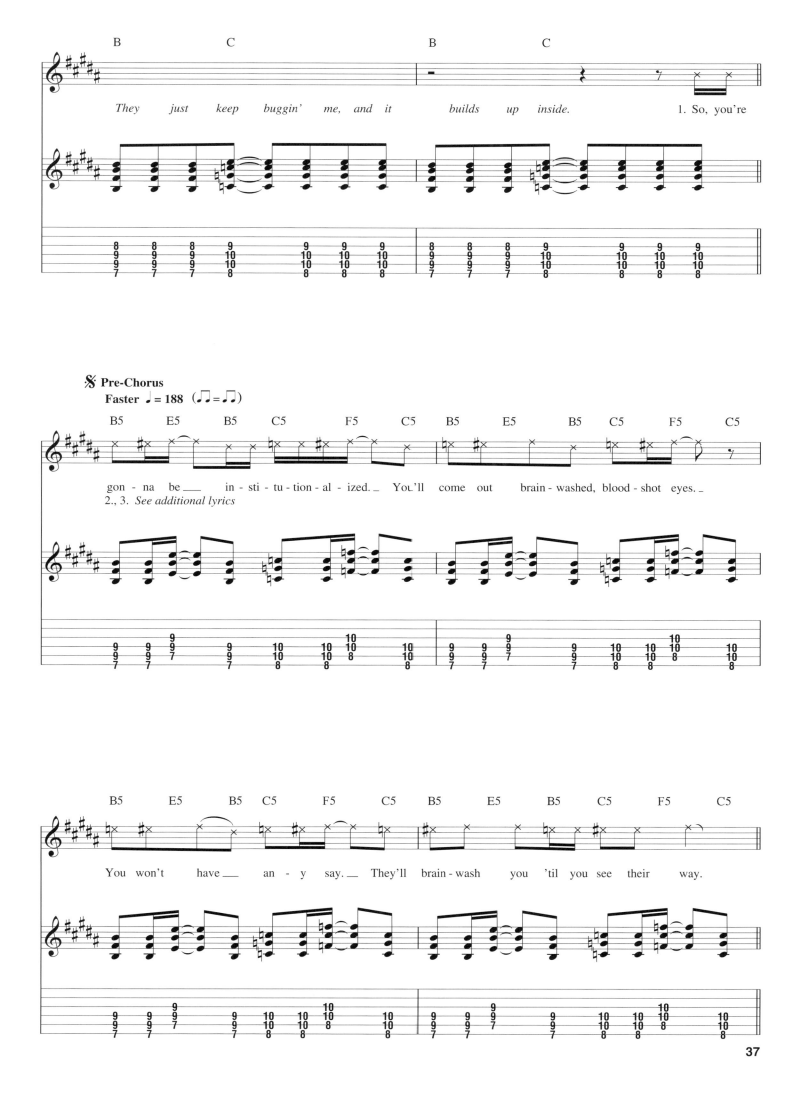

Chorus
Faster ♩ = 204

F#

I'm not cra - zy!

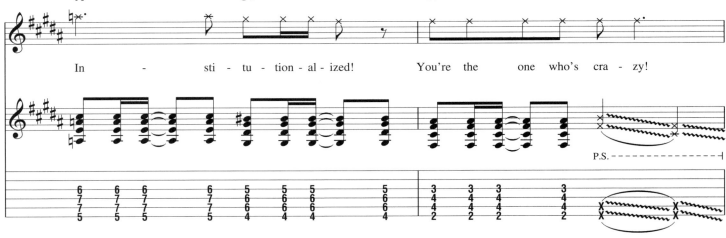

2nd time, substitute Fill 1

A   G#   F#

In - sti - tu - tion - al - ized!   You're the   one who's cra - zy!

P.S.

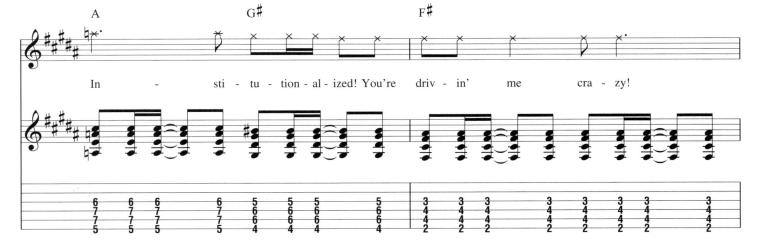

A   G#   F#

In - sti - tu - tion - al - ized! You're driv - in' me cra - zy!

Fill 1

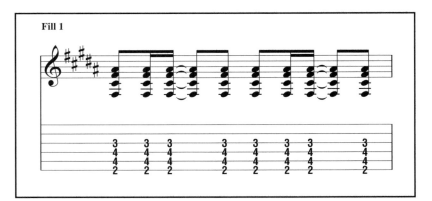

38

In - sti - tu - tion - al - ized! They stick me in___ an in - sti - tu - tion, and

said it was___ the on - ly so - lu - tion tc give me need - ed pro - fes - sion - al help to pro-

To Coda 1
To Coda 2

Slower ♩ = 126

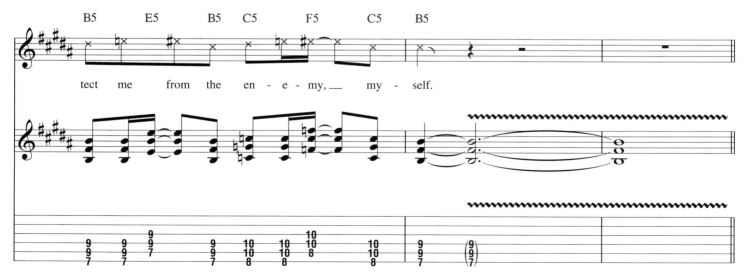

tect me from the en - e - my,___ my - self.

*Bend string behind the nut while continuing trill.

* Play as straight 8th notes.

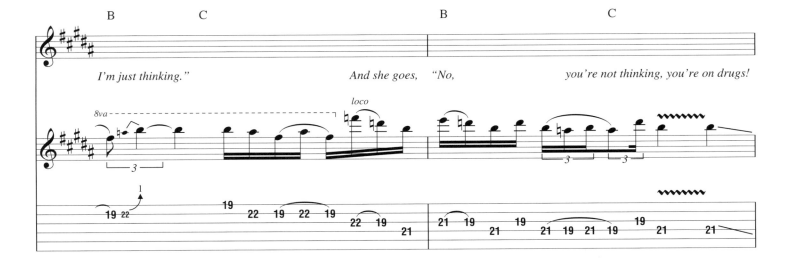

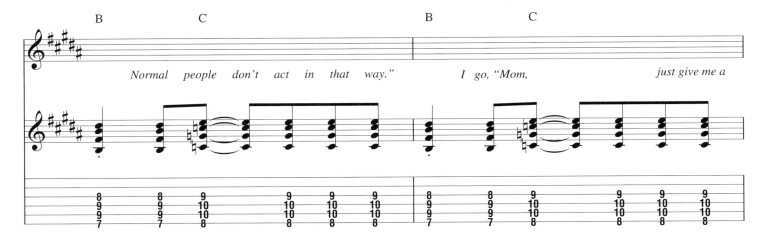

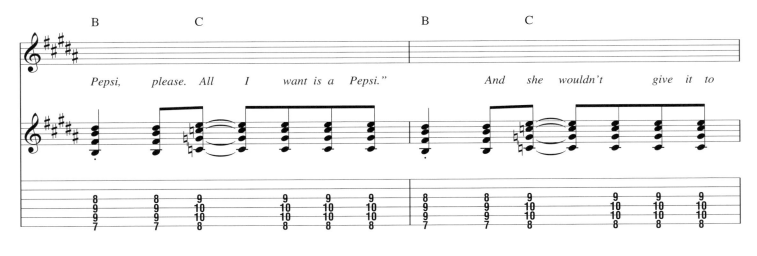

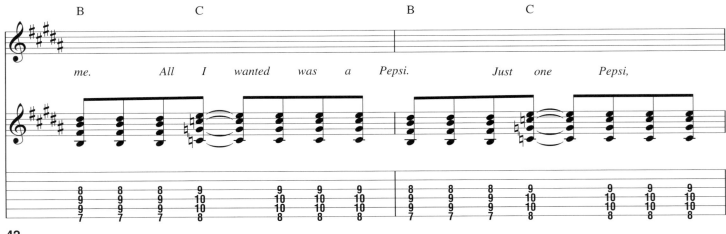

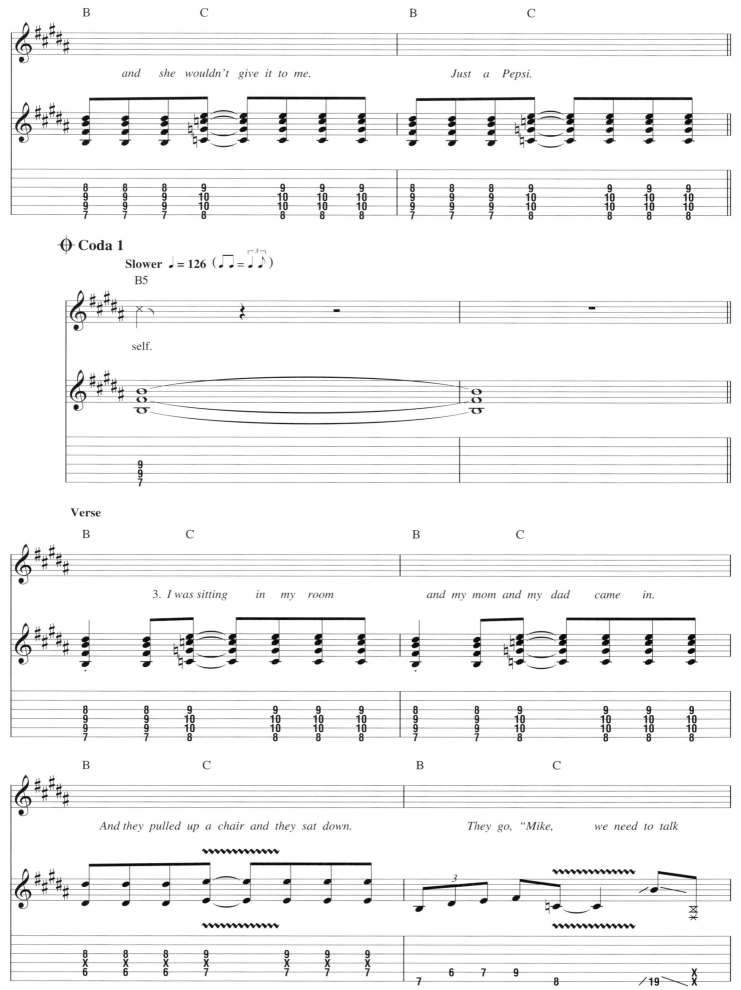

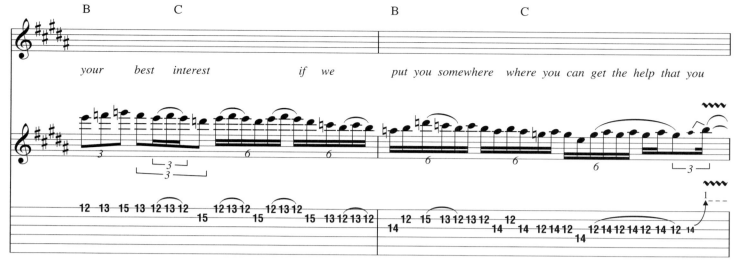

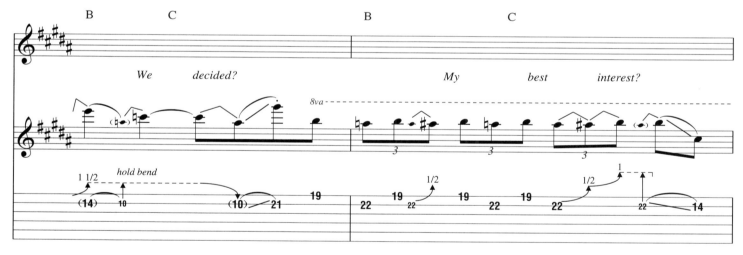

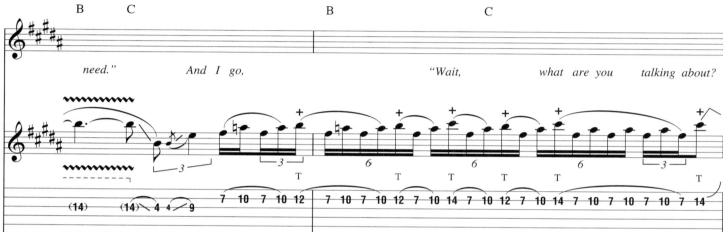

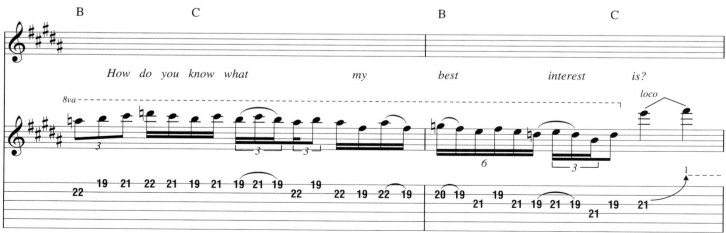

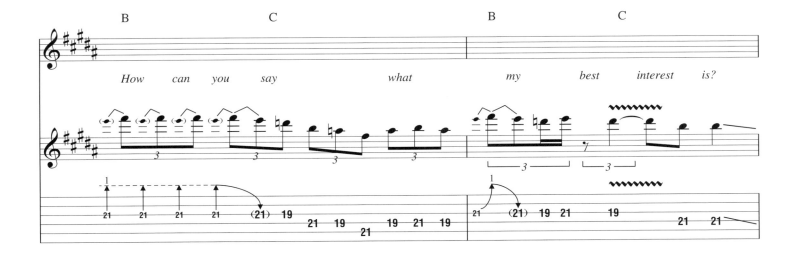

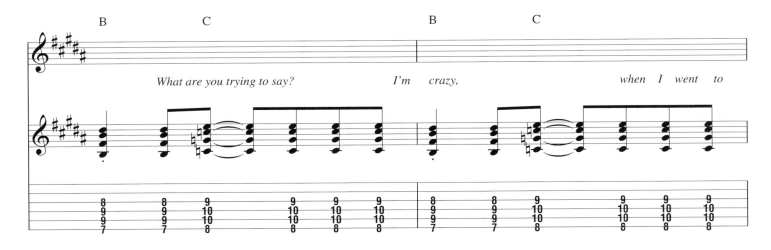

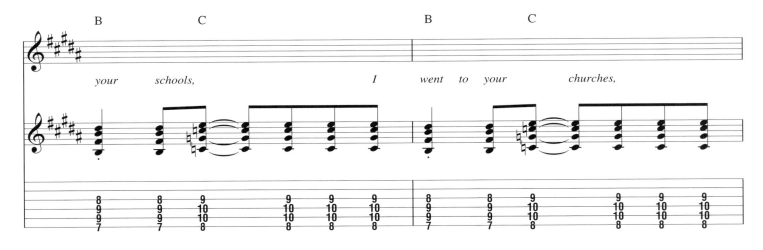

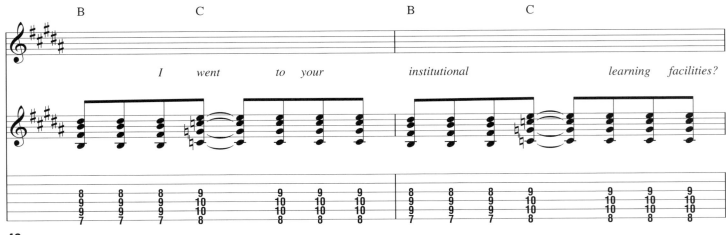

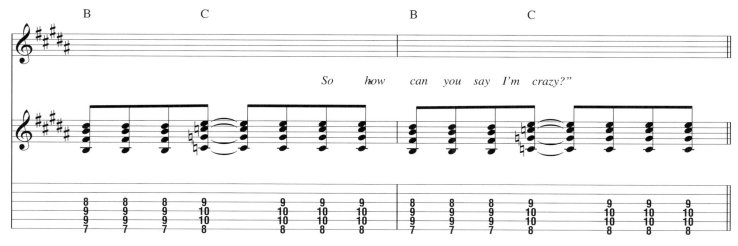

So how can you say I'm crazy?"

⊕ Coda 2

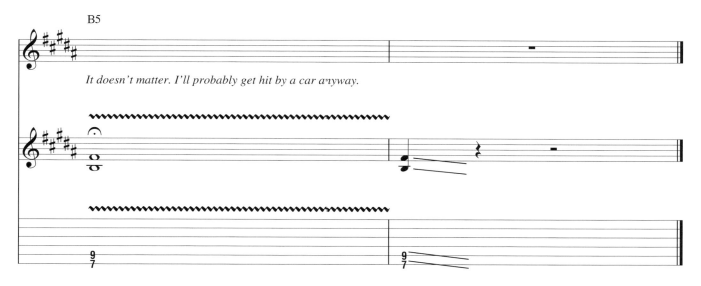

It doesn't matter. I'll probably get hit by a car anyway.

Additional Lyrics

Pre-Chorus 2. They give you a white shirt with long sleeves tied around your back, you're treated like thieves.
Drug you up because they're too lazy. It's too much work to help a crazy.

Pre-Chorus 3. They say they're gonna fix my brain, alleviate suffering and my pain.
By the time they fix my head, mentally I'll be dead.

London Calling

Words and Music by Joe Strummer, Mick Jones, Paul Simonon and Topper Headon

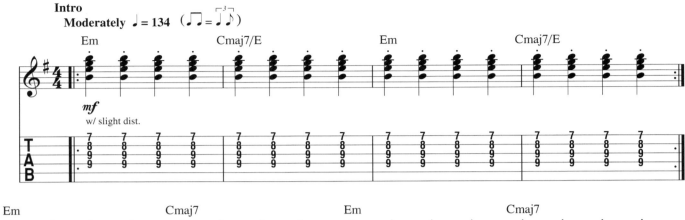

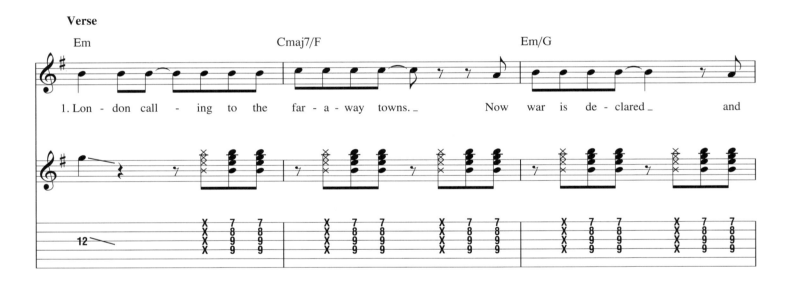

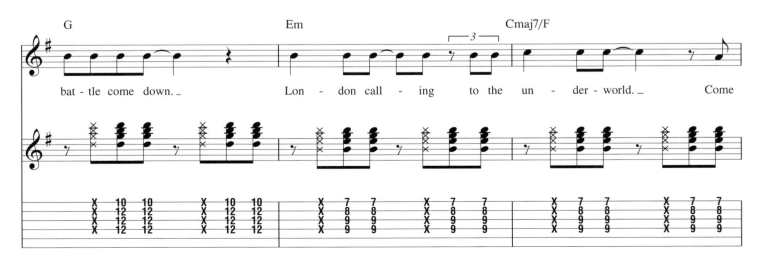

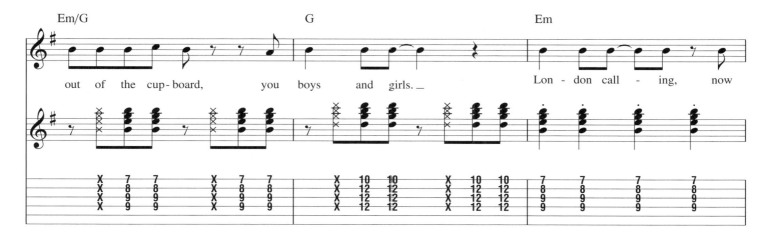

out of the cup-board, you boys and girls. Lon-don call - ing, now

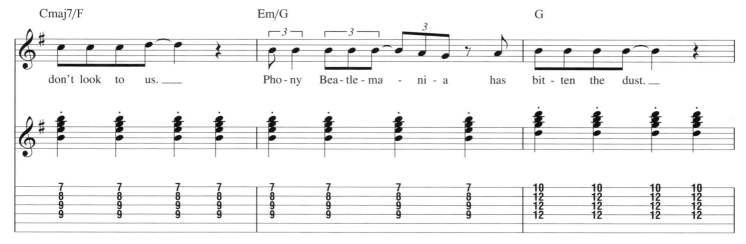

don't look to us. ___ Pho-ny Bea-tle-ma - ni - a has bit-ten the dust. ___

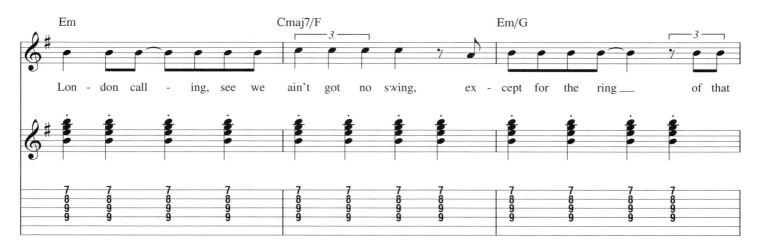

Lon-don call - ing, see we ain't got no swing, ex - cept for the ring ___ of that

§ **Chorus**

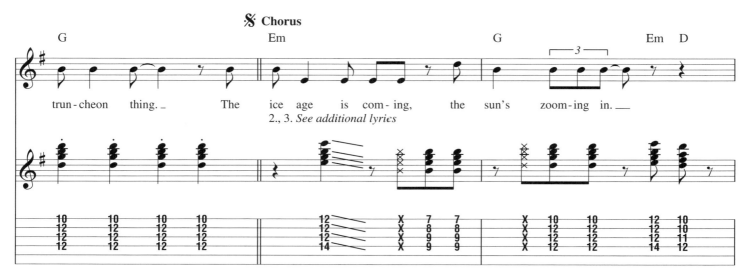

trun-cheon thing. ___ The ice age is com-ing, the sun's zoom-ing in. ___

2., 3. *See additional lyrics*

49

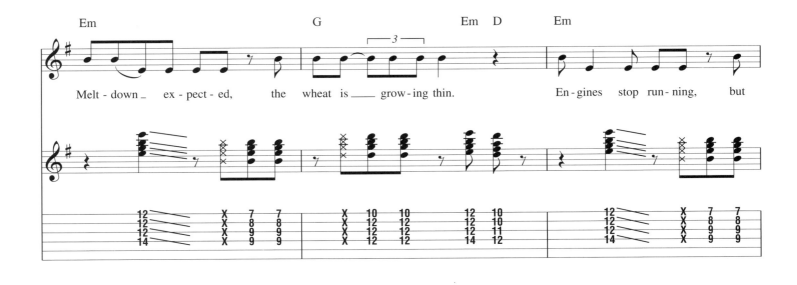

Melt - down __ ex - pect - ed, the wheat is __ grow - ing thin. En - gines stop run - ning, but

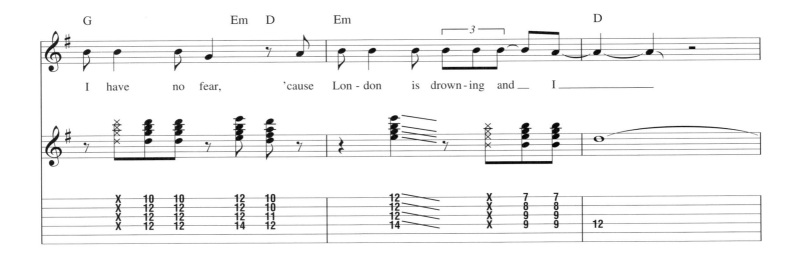

I have no fear, 'cause Lon - don is drown - ing and __ I _____

To Coda 1 ⊕
To Coda 2 ⊕

Verse

live by the riv - er. __ 2. Lon - don call - ing, to the im - i - ta - tion zone.

fdbk.

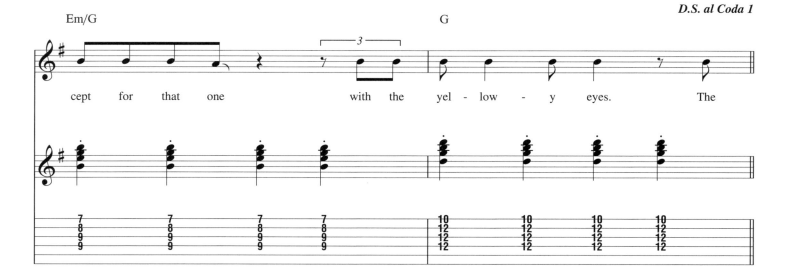

cept   for   that   one   with   the   yel - low - y   eyes.   The

Coda 1

Interlude

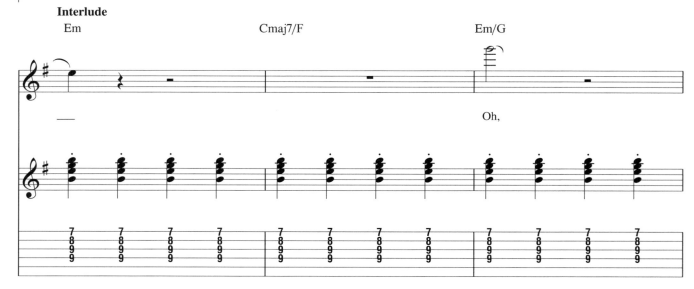

Oh,

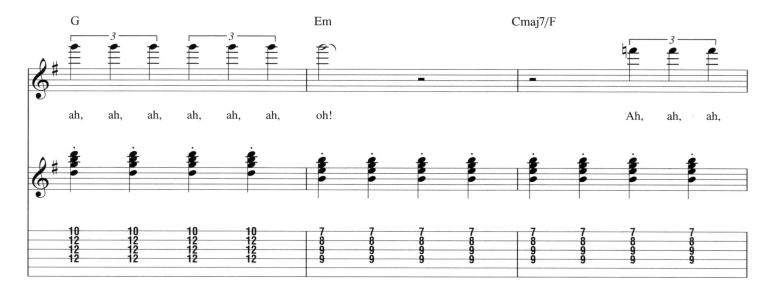

ah,   ah,   ah,   ah,   ah,   ah,   oh!   Ah,   ah,   ah,

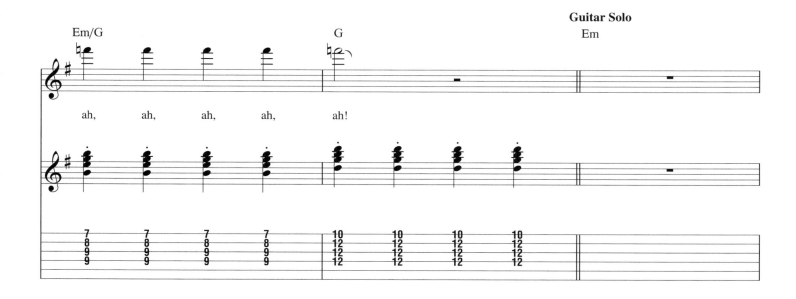

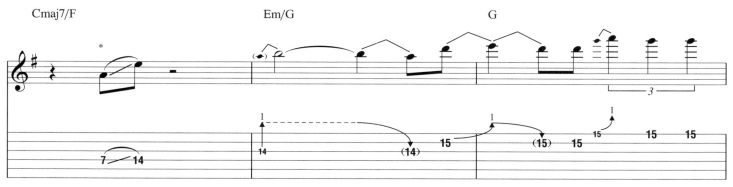

*Backwards guitar arranged for standard, next 7 meas.

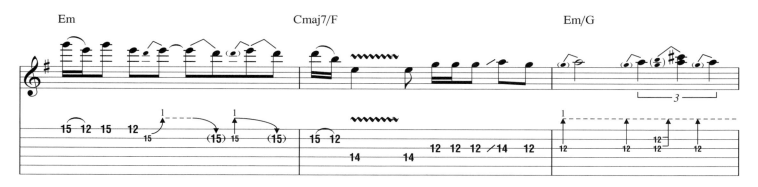

⊕ Coda 2

D.S. al Coda 2

Interlude

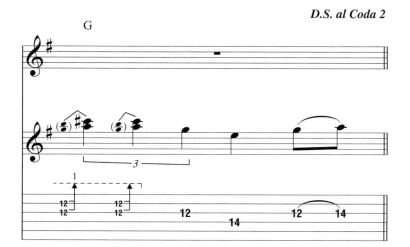

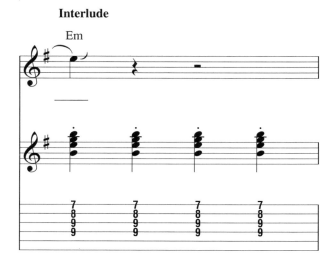

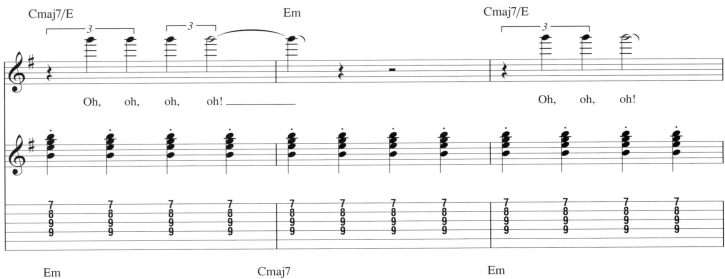

Oh, oh, oh, oh! _____ Oh, oh, oh!

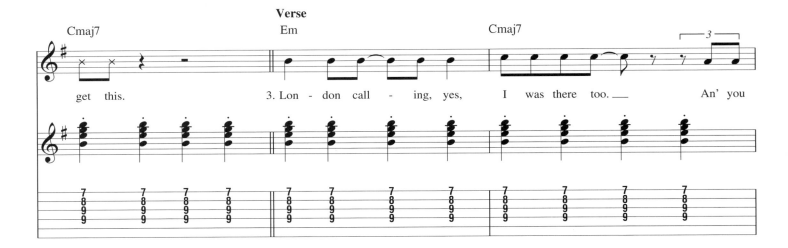

Now

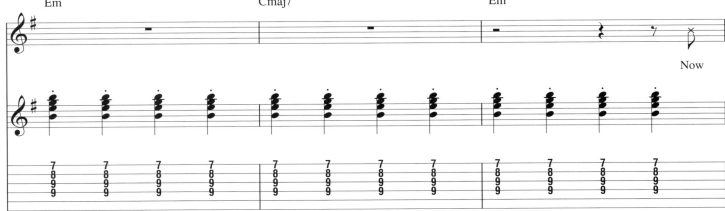

Verse

get this. 3. Lon - don call - ing, yes, I was there too. ___ An' you

know what they said? _ Well, some of it was true! _ Lon - don call - ing at the

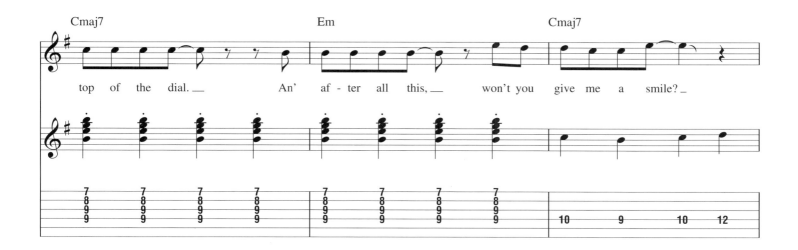

top of the dial. __ An' af-ter all this, __ won't you give me a smile? __

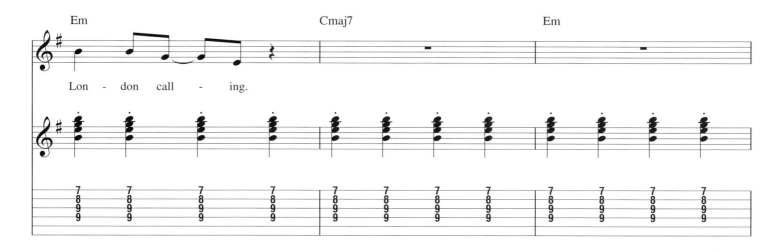

Lon - don call - ing.

I nev - er felt so much a, like...

Additional Lyrics

Chorus 2., 3. The ice age is coming, the sun's zooming in.
Engines stop running, the wheat is growing thin.
A nuclear error, but I have no fear,
'Cause London is drowning and I, I live by the river.

Orgasm Addict

Words and Music by Howard Devoto and Peter Shelley

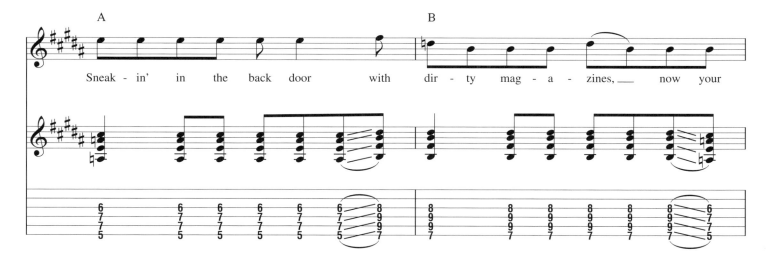

Sneak - in' in the back door with dir - ty mag - a - zines, ___ now your

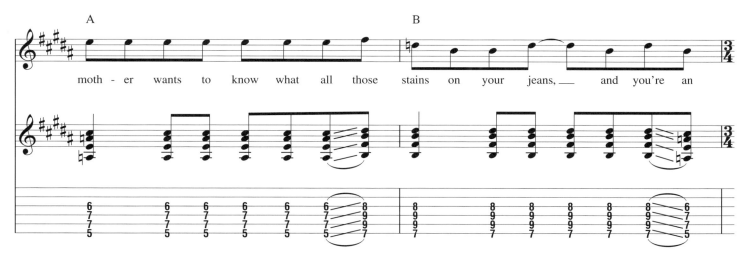

moth - er wants to know what all those stains on your jeans, ___ and you're an

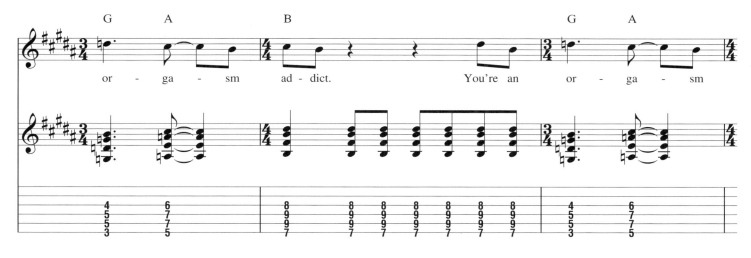

or - ga - sm ad - dict. You're an or - ga - sm

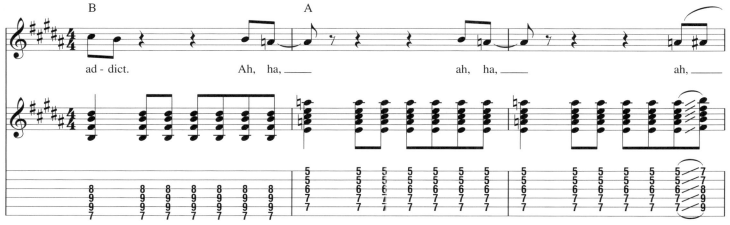

ad - dict. Ah, ha, ___ ah, ha, ___ ah, ___

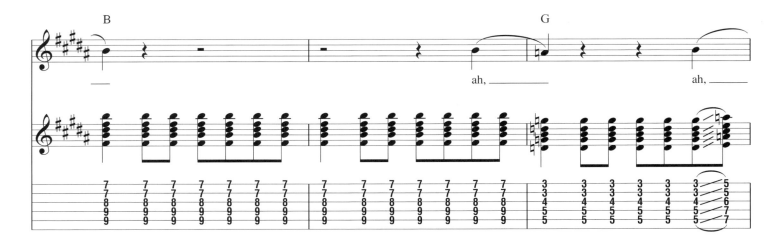

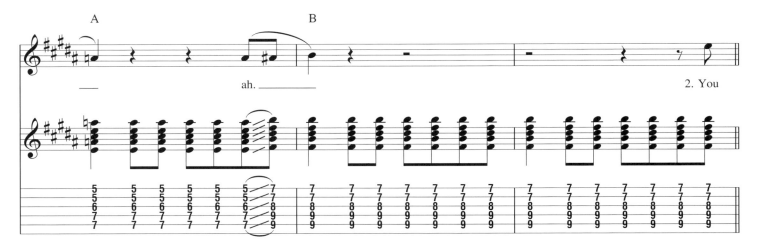

℅ Verse

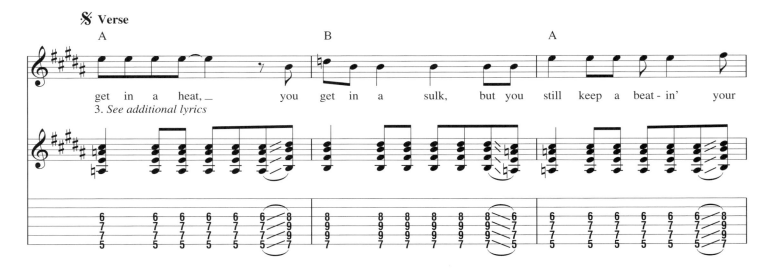

get in a heat, ___ you get in a sulk, but you still keep a beat-in' your
3. See additional lyrics

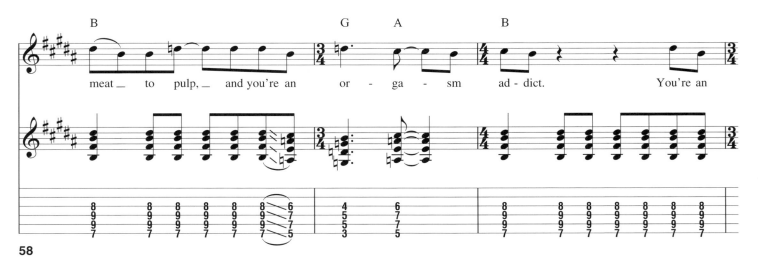

meat ___ to pulp, ___ and you're an or - ga - sm ad - dict. You're an

To Coda ⊕

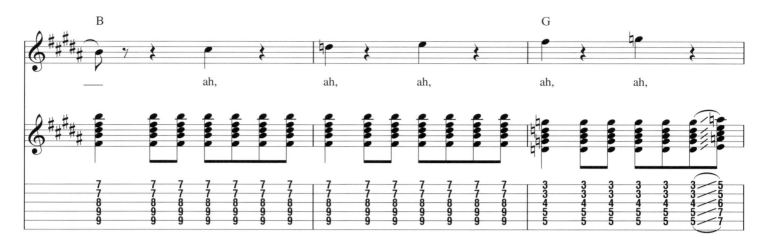

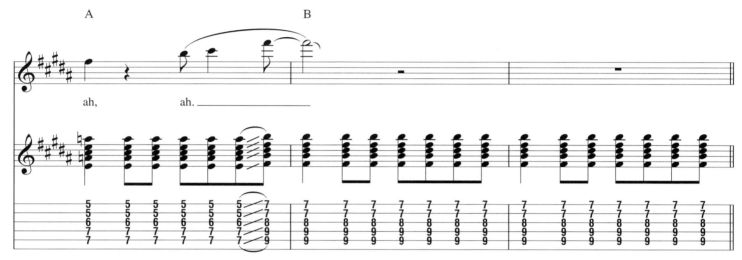

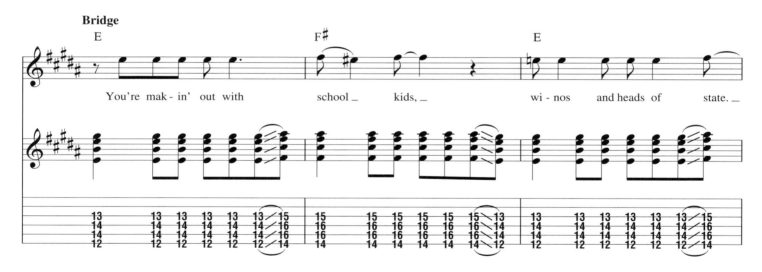

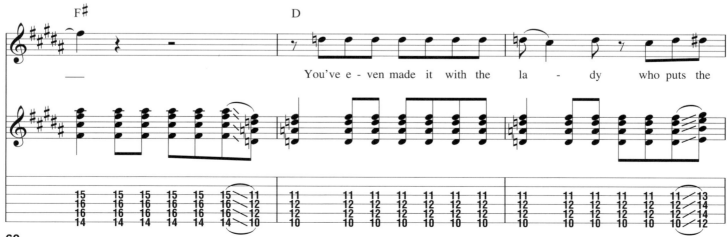

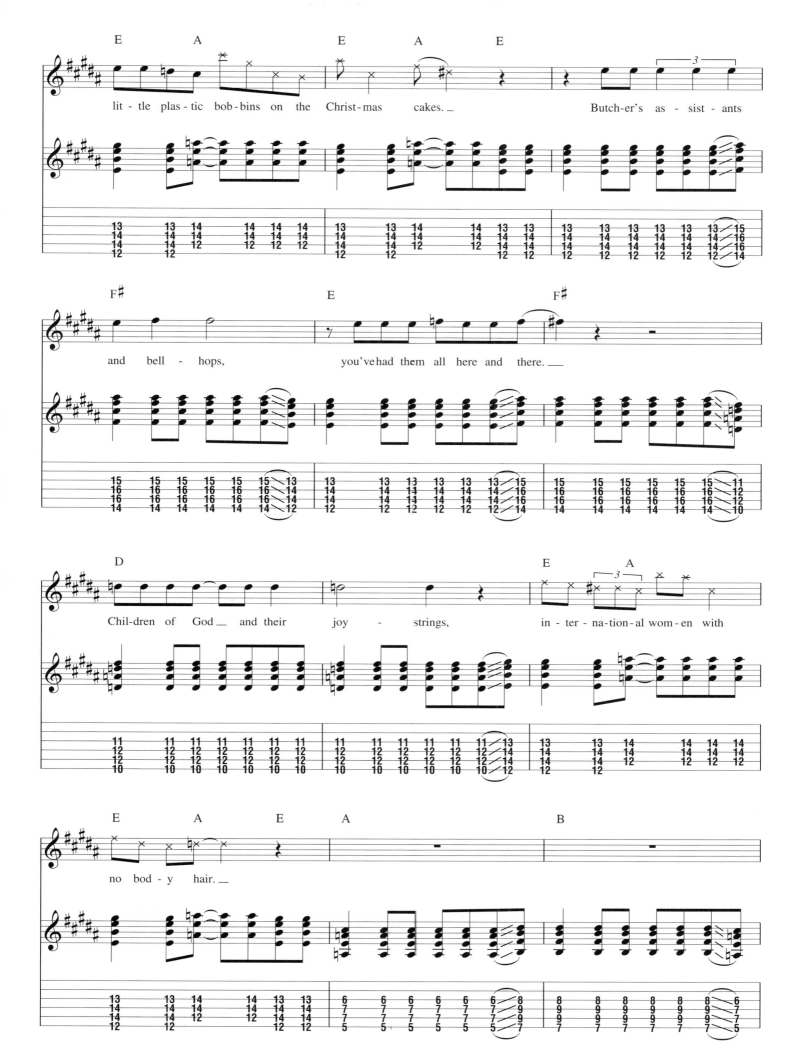

Additional Lyrics

3. Ooh, so well, you're askin' in an alley and your voice ain't steady.
   Your sex mechanic's rough, you're more than ready.
   You're an orgasm addict. You're an orgasm addict.
   Johnny want fuckie always and all ways.
   He's got the energy, he will amaze.
   He's an orgasm addict. He's an orgasm addict.

Search and Destroy

Words and Music by Iggy Pop and James Williamson

Intro

Moderately fast ♩ = 156

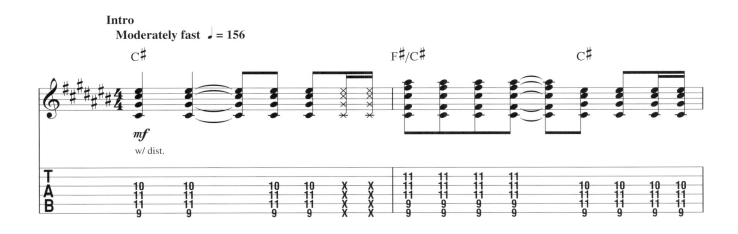

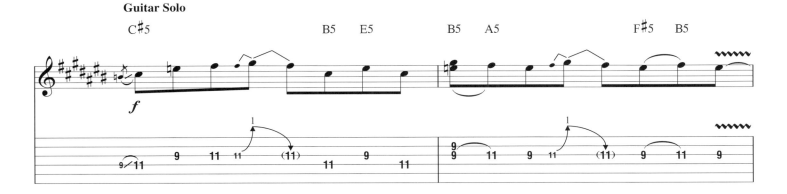

Guitar Solo

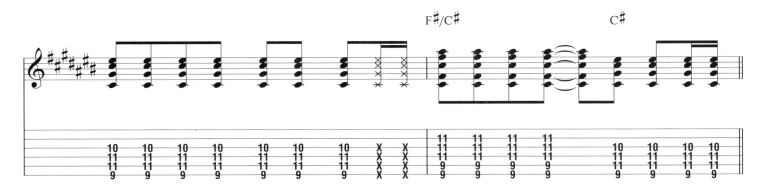

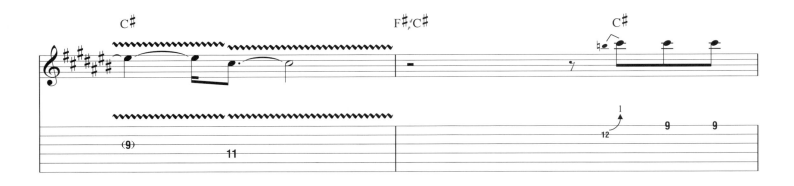

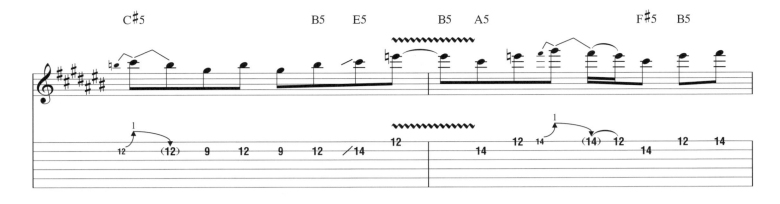

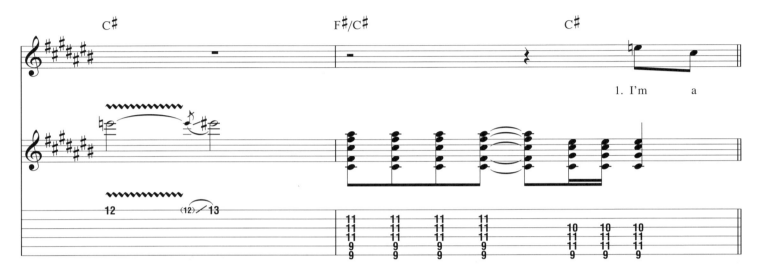

𝄋 Verse

street walk - in' chee - tah with a heart full of na - palm.____

2., 3. See additional lyrics

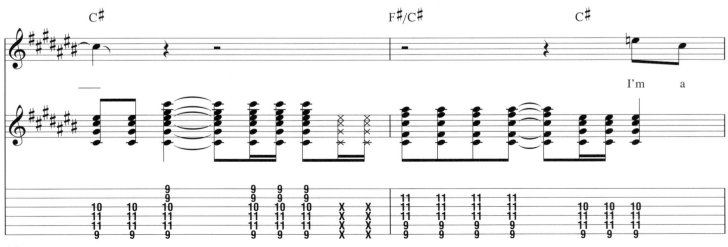

I'm a

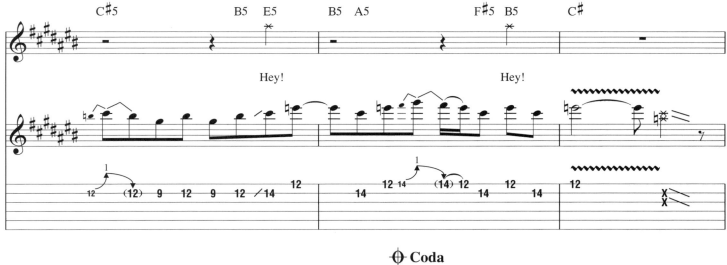

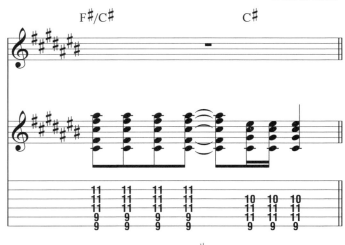

⊕ Coda

D.S. al Coda

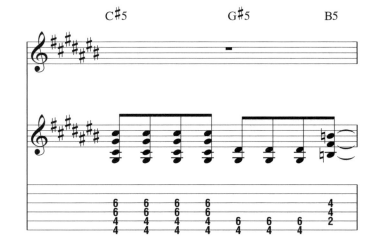

Chorus

And I'm the world's forgotten boy.

The one who's searchin', searchin' to destroy.

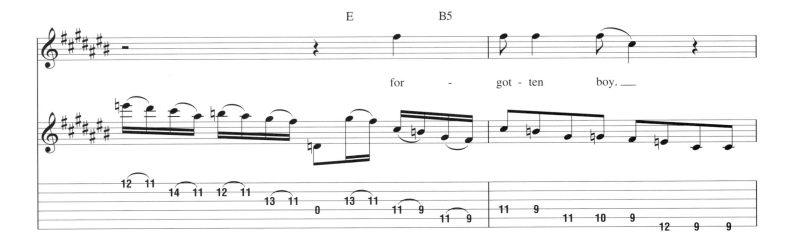

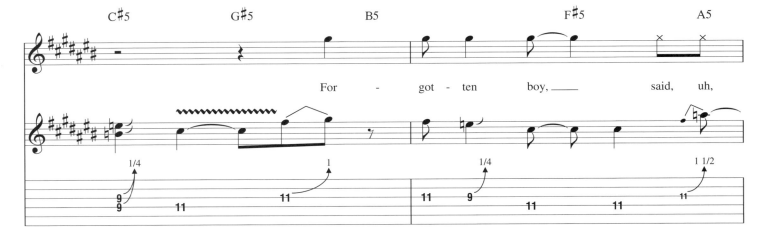

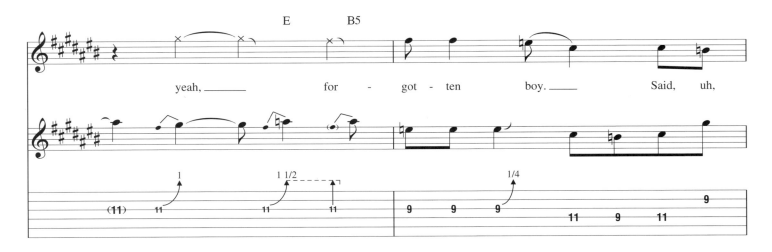

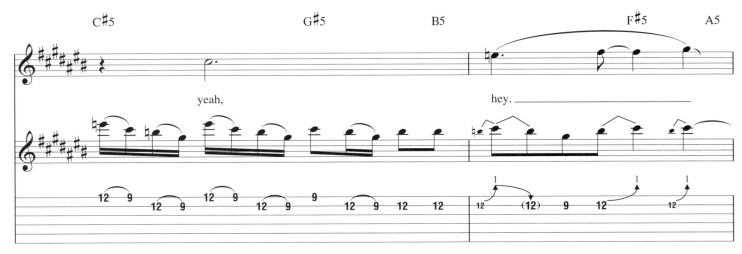

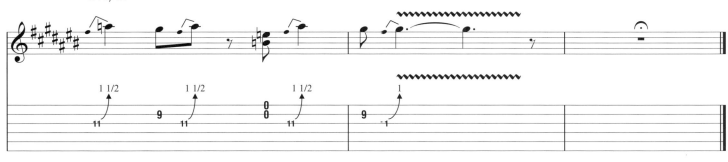

Additional Lyrics

2., 3. Look out honey, 'cause I'm usin' technology.
Ain't got time to make no apology.
Soul radiation in the dead of night.
Love in the middle of a firefight.

Pre-Chorus 2., 3. Honey, gotta strike me blind.
Somebody gotta save my soul.
Baby, penetrate my mind.

HAL·LEONARD GUITAR PLAY·ALONG

This series will help you play your favorite songs quickly and easily. Just follow the tab and listen to the CD to hear how the guitar should sound, and then play along using the separate backing tracks. Mac or PC users can also slow down the tempo without changing pitch by using the CD in their computer. The melody and lyrics are included in the book so that you can sing or simply follow along.

INCLUDES TAB

VOL. 1 – ROCK	00699570 / $16.99	
VOL. 2 – ACOUSTIC	00699569 / $16.95	
VOL. 3 – HARD ROCK	00699573 / $16.95	
VOL. 4 – POP/ROCK	00699571 / $16.99	
VOL. 5 – MODERN ROCK	00699574 / $16.99	
VOL. 6 – '90s ROCK	00699572 / $16.99	
VOL. 7 – BLUES	00699575 / $16.95	
VOL. 8 – ROCK	00699585 / $12.95	
VOL. 9 – PUNK ROCK	00699576 / $14.95	
VOL. 10 – ACOUSTIC	00699586 / $16.95	
VOL. 11 – EARLY ROCK	00699579 / $14.95	
VOL. 12 – POP/ROCK	00699587 / $14.95	
VOL. 13 – FOLK ROCK	00699581 / $14.95	
VOL. 14 – BLUES ROCK	00699582 / $16.95	
VOL. 15 – R&B	00699583 / $14.95	
VOL. 16 – JAZZ	00699584 / $15.95	
VOL. 17 – COUNTRY	00699588 / $15.95	
VOL. 18 – ACOUSTIC ROCK	00699577 / $15.95	
VOL. 19 – SOUL	00699578 / $14.95	
VOL. 20 – ROCKABILLY	00699580 / $14.95	
VOL. 21 – YULETIDE	00699602 / $14.95	
VOL. 22 – CHRISTMAS	00699600 / $15.95	
VOL. 23 – SURF	00699635 / $14.95	
VOL. 24 – ERIC CLAPTON	00699649 / $16.95	
VOL. 25 – LENNON & McCARTNEY	00699642 / $14.95	
VOL. 26 – ELVIS PRESLEY	00699643 / $14.95	
VOL. 27 – DAVID LEE ROTH	00699645 / $16.95	
VOL. 28 – GREG KOCH	00699646 / $14.95	
VOL. 29 – BOB SEGER	00699647 / $14.95	
VOL. 30 – KISS	00699644 / $14.95	
VOL. 31 – CHRISTMAS HITS	00699652 / $14.95	
VOL. 32 – THE OFFSPRING	00699653 / $14.95	
VOL. 33 – ACOUSTIC CLASSICS	00699656 / $16.95	
VOL. 34 – CLASSIC ROCK	00699658 / $16.95	
VOL. 35 – HAIR METAL	00699660 / $16.95	
VOL. 36 – SOUTHERN ROCK	00699661 / $16.95	
VOL. 37 – ACOUSTIC METAL	00699662 / $16.95	
VOL. 38 – BLUES	00699663 / $16.95	
VOL. 39 – '80s METAL	00699664 / $16.99	
VOL. 40 – INCUBUS	00699668 / $17.95	
VOL. 41 – ERIC CLAPTON	00699669 / $16.95	
VOL. 42 – CHART HITS	00699670 / $16.95	

VOL. 43 – LYNYRD SKYNYRD	00699681 / $17.95	
VOL. 44 – JAZZ	00699689 / $14.95	
VOL. 45 – TV THEMES	00699718 / $14.95	
VOL. 46 – MAINSTREAM ROCK	00699722 / $16.95	
VOL. 47 – HENDRIX SMASH HITS	00699723 / $19.95	
VOL. 48 – AEROSMITH CLASSICS	00699724 / $16.99	
VOL. 49 – STEVIE RAY VAUGHAN	00699725 / $16.95	
VOL. 50 – NÜ METAL	00699726 / $14.95	
VOL. 51 – ALTERNATIVE '90s	00699727 / $12.95	
VOL. 52 – FUNK	00699728 / $14.95	
VOL. 53 – DISCO	00699729 / $14.99	
VOL. 54 – HEAVY METAL	00699730 / $14.95	
VOL. 55 – POP METAL	00699731 / $14.95	
VOL. 56 – FOO FIGHTERS	00699749 / $14.95	
VOL. 57 – SYSTEM OF A DOWN	00699751 / $14.95	
VOL. 58 – BLINK-182	00699772 / $14.95	
VOL. 59 – GODSMACK	00699773 / $14.95	
VOL. 60 – 3 DOORS DOWN	00699774 / $14.95	
VOL. 61 – SLIPKNOT	00699775 / $14.95	
VOL. 62 – CHRISTMAS CAROLS	00699798 / $12.95	
VOL. 63 – CREEDENCE CLEARWATER REVIVAL	00699802 / $16.99	
VOL. 64 – THE ULTIMATE OZZY OSBOURNE	00699803 / $16.99	
VOL. 65 – THE DOORS	00699806 / $16.99	
VOL. 66 – THE ROLLING STONES	00699807 / $16.95	
VOL. 67 – BLACK SABBATH	00699808 / $16.99	
VOL. 68 – PINK FLOYD – DARK SIDE OF THE MOON	00699809 / $16.99	
VOL. 69 – ACOUSTIC FAVORITES	00699810 / $14.95	

VOL. 70 – OZZY OSBOURNE	00699805 / $16.99	
VOL. 71 – CHRISTIAN ROCK	00699824 / $14.95	
VOL. 72 – ACOUSTIC '90S	00699827 / $14.95	
VOL. 73 – BLUESY ROCK	00699829 / $16.99	
VOL. 74 – PAUL BALOCHE	00699831 / $14.95	
VOL. 75 – TOM PETTY	00699882 / $16.99	
VOL. 76 – COUNTRY HITS	00699884 / $14.95	
VOL. 78 – NIRVANA	00700132 / $14.95	
VOL. 80 – ACOUSTIC ANTHOLOGY	00700175 / $19.95	
VOL. 81 – ROCK ANTHOLOGY	00700176 / $22.99	
VOL. 82 – EASY SONGS	00700177 / $12.99	
VOL. 83 – THREE CHORD SONGS	00700178 / $12.99	
VOL. 84 – STEELY DAN	00700200 / $16.99	
VOL. 86 – BOSTON	00700465 / $16.99	
VOL. 87 – ACOUSTIC WOMEN	00700763 / $14.99	
VOL. 88 – GRUNGE	00700467 / $16.99	
VOL. 96 – THIRD DAY	00700560 / $14.95	
VOL. 97 – ROCK BAND	00700703 / $14.99	
VOL. 98 – ROCK BAND	00700704 / $14.95	
VOL. 99 – ZZ TOP	00700762 / $14.99	
VOL. 100 – B.B. KING	00700466 / $14.99	
VOL. 103 – SWITCHFOOT	00700773 / $16.99	
VOL. 106 – WEEZER	00700958 / $14.99	
VOL. 108 – THE WHO	00701053 / $14.99	
VOL. 109 – STEVE MILLER	00701054 / $14.99	
VOL. 111 – JOHN MELLENCAMP	00701056 / $14.99	
VOL. 113 – JIM CROCE	00701058 / $14.99	
VOL. 114 – BON JOVI	00701060 / $14.99	
VOL. 115 – JOHNNY CASH	00701070 / $14.99	
VOL. 116 – THE VENTURES	00701124 / $14.99	
VOL. 119 – AC/DC CLASSICS	00701356 / $14.99	

Complete song lists available online.

Prices, contents, and availability subject to change without notice.

FOR MORE INFORMATION, SEE YOUR LOCAL MUSIC DEALER, OR WRITE TO:

HAL·LEONARD®
CORPORATION
7777 W. BLUEMOUND RD. P.O. BOX 13819 MILWAUKEE, WI 53213

Visit Hal Leonard online at www.halleonard.com